A MAN IN A

A MAN IN A HURRY:

The Extraordinary Life & Times

of

Edward Payson Weston,

The World's Greatest Walker

by

Nick Harris, Helen Harris

and Paul Marshall

Published by deCoubertin Books Ltd in 2012.
deCoubertin Books, PO Box 65170, London, SE18 9HB
www.decoubertin.co.uk
First hardback edition.
ISBN: 0956431372
ISBN-13: 978-0956431370

A CIP catalogue record for this book is available from the British Library.
Cover by Zoran Lucic
Typeset design by www.allenmohr.com

Printed and bound by Korotan.

For Daisy and Isabel,

who would have preferred a puppy.

CHAPTERS

PROLOGUE

Five hundred thousand people crammed New York's greatest
thoroughfare today to see one white-haired man march through their
cheering lines. The man was Edward P. Weston, and the ovation
which he received was the greatest ever accorded to any
man not connected with public life.

Portsmouth Daily Herald,
New Hampshire, 3 May 1910

EDWARD PAYSON WESTON'S 3,100-MILE WALK from California to New York, completed on 3 May 1910, was one of his great achievements, but only one. It took him just 77 days — and he was 71 years old at the time.

For half a century he had been one of the most famous people in America, indeed in the English-speaking world, as the first age of international celebrity unfolded. Largely forgotten today, his exploits were covered by millions of words in hundreds of newspapers and magazines. He was a 'big-name athlete' and a 'star performer' before either of those phrases had been coined.

And how had he gained such widespread fame? By walking.

Astonishing though it might sound today, in the decades before the dawn of the 20th century, professional walking was among the most popular spectator sports in the United States, Britain and other nations. At one stage it was probably the biggest draw in the world, with hundreds of thousands of people attending events.

Pedestrianism as a discipline had attracted some attention in earlier times via individual eccentrics. Robert Barclay Allardice, a Scottish laird and military man, walked a mile per hour for 1,000 hours in 1809 to some acclaim, for example.

But the mass interest in match racing in the late 19th century was of an entirely different magnitude. These were no ordinary days out. They went on for five days, six days, seven days of non-stop walking, most often on wooden or cinder tracks laid down inside cavernous halls or markets.

Think about the last time that you went for a five-mile walk. What about ten miles? Or 20 or 50? Quite probably you have never walked that far in one go.

The biggest names of the great age of pedestrianism would walk 500 miles and more, around and around a track until some of them literally dropped, their feet a mess and their bodies drained. Massive crowds paid good money to come along and watch, for an hour or a day or the whole of an event, and to drink and smoke — and to gamble on the outcome.

Money was a big ingredient in the phenomenon. Walkers raced for enormous cash prizes, and more money still was wagered on who won. More often than not, when it mattered, Edward Weston won.

His long, extraordinary and often controversial life ran from the Gold Rush to the Jazz Age, through the reign of Queen Victoria and beyond. He worked in journalism and publishing and above all self-promotion, mainly through his walking, travelling widely across America and Great Britain.

P.T. Barnum, the legendary circus promoter, was his contemporary and friend, as were other prominent showmen, musicians, writers, businessmen and politicians.

It was Abraham Lincoln who unknowingly set Weston on the road to fame. Weston lost a bet with a friend on the outcome of the 1860 US Presidential election, which Lincoln won. Weston's forfeit was to walk 478 miles from Boston to Washington to attend Lincoln's inauguration.

He completed the journey in ten days and subsequently became a prime mover in pedestrianism, the sport that took the Victorian world by storm.

On his first trip to England, in 1876, he brought the astounding properties of cocaine to the attention of a fascinated British medical establishment for the first time. That episode caused a furore but it was exercise, healthy food, plenty of rest and lashings of whisky (on his feet, not down his throat) that played a greater part in Weston's success than any narcotic.

After one 5,000-mile walk around Britain in 1884, physicians from the Royal Society concluded, 'his feat is the greatest recorded labour that any human being has ever undertaken without injury'.

His private life was no less dramatic, a consequence of a character flawed by the obsessions that drove him. Weston, aka 'The Wily Wobbler' for his sprightly gait, was a family man, married with three children . He was forever concocting schemes to make them rich.

But he was also a dandy, a charmer, a hit with the ladies who flocked to see him. His roving eye eventually led to the break-up of his marriage, to at least one illegitimate child, and mortal danger.

This is his story.

CHAPTER 1

NEW ENGLAND BOY

EDWARD PAYSON WESTON BECAME FAMOUS for amazing stamina and endurance, for his ability to keep walking while his competitors staggered and fell, but what really set him apart from his rivals was his power of recovery. He could walk 80 miles without stopping, keep on moving to the very point of collapse, rest for 20 minutes and then bounce back, bright as a button and ready for more. From the start of his long life, Weston was a natural at bouncing back.

Weston was born in Providence, Rhode Island, on 15 March 1839, the second child of Silas, a teacher and merchant, and Maria, a housewife and writer. He may have been born early, in a hurry already, because baby Edward weighed just four pounds. The child was not expected to live. The story told by his daughter Lillian was that 'he was so frail and delicate that the nurse was obliged to carry him on a pillow'.

Infant mortality was of course commonplace; one in four American babies in the 1830s died before they reached their first birthday. For the parents of such a tiny baby as Edward, more than two pounds below the average birth weight even then, the chances of

13

celebrating a birthday with him must have seemed frighteningly small. But the fragile mite on the cushion was stronger than he looked, and in the first challenge of his life, Weston was the winner.

Survival against the odds had been written into Edward's family tree long before he was. His father had been born on 9 March 1804 to James and Betsey Weston of Francestown, New Hampshire, little more than 100 miles from Plymouth, Massachusetts, where James Weston's family had landed in the 17th century. Two of James's ancestors — his 'five-greats' grandfather Richard Warren and 'four-greats' grandfather Francis Cooke — were among the 105 passengers who crossed the Atlantic on board the Mayflower in 1620.

Francis Cooke had been a member of the Leyden Community of pilgrims and both men signed the Mayflower Compact, binding the group in allegiance to King James and to each other. While only five of 149 people on the Mayflower died during the voyage, the New England winter proved a greater trial than the journey and half of the crew and passengers perished during their first bitter season in the New World.

Richard Warren and Francis Cooke survived and soon their families sailed to join them in the colony. In 1625, Richard's wife Elizabeth and their five daughters arrived on the Anne. The Warrens had two more (American-born) children before Richard's death in 1628, and all seven children lived to have large families of their own. Generations of Hannahs, Marys, Marthas, Josephs, Seths and Johns were born, married, bred and died in Massachusetts and New Hampshire. They lived as traders, farmers and coopers and did not stray far from Plymouth. Their thousands of descendants included Presidents Ulysses Grant and Franklin Roosevelt and writers Henry Wadsworth Longfellow and Laura Ingalls Wilder, as well as young Edward Payson Weston.

Francis Cooke's wife Hester sailed with their younger son Jacob (the elder, John, having crossed with his father) and the couple had three daughters born during the 1620s. Three of Francis and Hester's children survived and their descendants included Orson Welles and several Beach Boys. To add to the Weston clan's connections, another English ancestor, John Churchill, links the family to Winston Churchill and the English royal family.

Around 20 million contemporary Americans and millions of Britons can trace a direct lineage to Richard Warren and Francis Cooke, and hence could trace their own relationship to Weston.

A little more than 200 years after the Mayflower landing, EPW was born, a New Englander to his bones, strengthened by those survivors' genes passed down the years from Richard and Elizabeth and Francis and Hester.

The frail baby grew into healthy boyhood but in his teenage years some illness made Weston a virtual invalid and his friends feared that he was suffering from consumption. He recovered from that setback too, but became a small, slightly built man. He never looked like an athlete, journalists noting his odd shape, like a 'baked potato stuck with two toothpicks' according to one. But another reporter wrote that beneath Weston's mild appearance was hidden the 'grit of the Spartan'.

Edward's father was another man whose appearance was at odds with his nature. A large man, six feet four inches tall, his size belied a rather dreamy, artistic temperament; Silas played the viol and wrote poetry. Edward's mother Maria was a delicate-looking, intelligent woman who wrote romantic but moralistic poetry and novels. Silas and Maria handed their fondness for writing not only to Edward, who became a journalist in his twenties and still wrote for newspapers into his seventies, but to his eldest daughter Lillian as well. She was another journalist and also sold short stories to magazines, mostly thinly disguised autobiographical tales.

Lillian's granddaughter Joyce Litz is a writer too and has written a book about her grandmother. The Montana Frontier tells the story of Lillian's upbringing with a famous father, her journalism and her later struggle to make a life on a Montana ranch. In the book, Joyce described Silas and Maria Weston as an unusual couple, and wrote that with such parents 'it's not surprising Weston had an unusual approach to life'. Weston would often seem to be pulled in two directions, between his mother's correctness and his father's fancy. In his career, he walked a tightrope between two competing wishes: to be respected and to avoid dull respectability and routine.

At the time of Edward's birth, Silas was leading a perfectly ordinary life as the head of his household and principal of the 3rd District School in downtown Providence. He had taken a teaching job at the school in 1830 and became principal two years later, around the same time as the couple's eldest child Ellen was born.

In 1841, a year after the birth of a third baby, Mary Anna Jane, Silas left teaching to open a 'variety' store on the corner of Pine and Parsonage Streets, only to return to the schoolroom a few years later after the arrival in 1846 of the couple's last child, a son called Emmons.

During these early years of their family life, Maria managed to combine caring for her young family and her home with writing. In 1847 she published two long poems and a short story. The next year, she published a book, The Weldron Family, or Vicissitudes of Fortune, under the name Marie De France, printed by Weedon and Peek of Providence. The book recounts the lives of several generations of the 'Weldrons', descendants of the Mayflower Pilgrims. The preface of the book describes it as 'an unvarnished statement of facts', and indicates that 'the surnames vary somewhat from the original'. The book then is Maria's version of the Weston family's history, and she views her husband and children as the descendants of an extraordinary generation, 'the dauntless, noble-spirited, and energetic few, who came to this savage wilderness to enjoy, untrammeled, that great and inestimable blessing, liberty of conscience'.

A year after the publication of The Weldron Family, when Edward was ten years old, it seems that the energetic spirit of his fore-fathers took hold of Silas and he again turned his back on teaching, this time for good.

Gold had been discovered in the hills of California in 1848 and tens of thousands of people flooded into the West from Europe and Asia, as well as from the settled eastern states of America, hoping to make a fortune. For Silas, however, the decision to board a ship to San Francisco seemed to be inspired more by a dream of America's wilderness than by the chance to dig up riches and make his family secure. He would be gone for three years and eventually came back, not with a sack of gold nuggets or even a pocketful of dollars, but with the story of his adventures among the sublime landscapes and frightening wildlife, the Indians and gamblers of the Wild West.

And, with his father gone in search of the Wild West experience, Edward's life changed too. It was time for his adventures to begin.

SILAS'S DEPARTURE LEFT MARIA ALONE with four children, by then aged seventeen, ten, eight and three, and only the money from her books to keep them all. Some months after Silas's departure, a touring band called the Hutchinson Family Singers visited Rhode Island, and Edward Weston, the eldest son, man of the house in his father's absence, got himself a job.

In 1862, Weston published a pamphlet, titled 'The Pedestrian', which as well as giving a detailed account of his walk to Washington the year before, included a brief memoir of his young life. (Confusingly, he wrote about himself in both the first and the third person.) In this memoir, he recalled: 'During the winter of 1849, the Hutchinson Family visited Providence, and young Weston urged his mother to allow him to accompany them on their travels. His mother being in feeble health, thought they would be good guardians for him, and gave her consent. He travelled with them for a year, selling candies and song-books at their concerts.'

Whether Maria's 'feeble health' was a physical illness or the manifestation of her distress at being left alone with four children, letting Edward go on the road with the Hutchinsons at least left her with one less mouth to feed for the year, and probably he would have sent money home too. The Hutchinson Family was not any old collection of travelling musicians. They were the most famous and successful American musical group of the 19th century and toured the States for decades, at one time making $1000 per performance, something like the average annual middle-class salary. The group was openly political; their close-harmony songs were anti-slavery, pro-temperance and pro-women's rights. One of their best-known songs, 'Get off the Track', was set to the tune of 'Old Dan Tucker', which had been made famous in 1843 by the blackface troupe the Virginia Minstrels. The Hutchinsons turned it into a protest song against slavery, an abolitionist battle-cry.

After his year on the road, Edward spent another 18 months living with Jesse Hutchinson and going to school in Boston. He paid his board by selling sweets at the city's Ordway Hall theatre, the home of a blackface minstrel troupe, Ordway's Aeolians.

The day Edward left Providence with the Hutchinsons, he lost his taste for the ordinary. His new life, on the road and in the theatre, was an unusual one for a boy from a middle-class New England family. And this unlikely turn in young Edward's path had a lasting effect. For one thing, he grew up to share at least some of the Hutchinsons' views: while there is no record of Weston's opinions on the slave trade, he was a lifelong advocate for temperance and, as a father, pushed his daughters to seek independence.

Furthermore, those months at the fringes of his hosts' celebrity gave him a taste for fame and a talent for sales; at the end of those two and a half years selling sweets and song-books, he went home quite the young entrepreneur. Most of all the experience spoiled him for ordinary life; from the age of 12, Weston sought movement and excitement, and resisted routine.

In 1852, both Weston men returned to Providence. Silas was full of the sights and adventures of the Wild West. He turned his diaries into a pamphlet, 'Four Months in the Mines of California, or Life in the Mountains'. The 13-year-old Edward, the young businessman, published the book in 1853 and then hawked it door-to-door in nearby towns and villages.

Silas's account of his ultimately unsuccessful and rather half-hearted hunt for gold conjures up a sentimental character, a dreamer who weeps regularly and scares himself silly by imagining bears and Red Indians behind every bush and boulder. One night he mistook a miner carrying an umbrella for a grizzly on the prowl and almost got the man shot. His only real encounters with Native Americans were peaceful, even friendly, including a brief, mimed chat with a small family group − mother, father, grandfather and a young boy − he found gathering herbs in the mountains.

These were probably Paiute Indians, 150,000 of whom lived a quiet, pastoral life in California, subsisting on roots and insects. Silas was disgusted to hear of a group of miners near Auburn who had ambushed and massacred 30 Native Americans, men, women and children, supposedly in retaliation for the shooting of one of their colleagues. Attacks like this became widespread and the Californian Paiute were virtually wiped out by the miners.

Silas made nothing from gold-digging, at one point he was even in debt, but he was there for the experience more than the opportunity to get rich. Luckily, with Edward's help, he had more success as a writer. At 15 cents per copy, Silas's 46-page booklet was popular enough to run into a second edition in 1854.

That same year, Edward took another job, this time selling news-papers on the Boston, Providence and Stonington Railroad. Soon after, he moved to a steamer, the Empire State, which sailed up the coast from

New York to Fall River, Massachusetts, where passengers could catch a train to Boston. His father, however, ordered Edward to return to Providence, where the teenager spent six months as a merchant's clerk. Then Silas apprenticed the boy to a local jeweller, but Edward did not like the work; he did not care for being stuck in one place and there was no pay, so he convinced his father to let him quit.

According to his great-granddaughter Joyce Litz, it was at this time, when Edward was 15, that the future athlete became 'a semi-invalid'. He had been healthy enough until then to travel and work, so presumably he suffered some illness; his friends thought it was tuberculosis.

The Westons moved to Boston where a family friend, who was a sports coach, asked if he could work with Edward to improve his health, which meant taking him off coffee and putting him on a strict diet of vegetables and milk. The friend got the boy to take a short walk each day, gradually increasing the distance, and soon Weston started to enjoy his strolls and recovered his strength.

The next year, 1855, Edward published another of his father's pamphlets: a record of a trip to the Azores. This time, Silas had gone with the explicit aim of gathering material for a book, but this one failed to find an audience and Edward left home again to look for paid work. In his memoir, he wrote that in the spring of 1856, aged 17, he joined a circus but was quickly fired.

Weston explains that he was hit by lightning while riding in a wagon near Tyngsborough, Massachusetts, and that a few days later, when the circus was performing in Boston, he felt too ill to appear and was dismissed. It seems a far-fetched tale, impossible to confirm, but it is impossible to refute too. People do get struck by lightning, and just because Weston was a daydreamer, that does not mean he made the story up.

From there, the memoir continues, he fled to Canada and joined the famous Spalding and Rogers Circus in Quebec. Spalding and Rogers was one of the largest and best-known American circuses. The company pioneered the use of boats as both transport and performance space: its 'Floating Palace' seated 3,400 spectators and was towed by a steamboat that also had a stage of its own. (In 1857, the company became one of the first to travel by train, and in 1858 Abraham Lincoln and Stephen A. Douglas held debates in the company's 'leviathan' tent, which could hold audiences of up to 4,000, during their battle for the Illinois senatorship.) Weston joined the circus as a drummer and was taken under the wing of celebrated bugler Edward Kendall, the 'magic bugler', who taught the boy to play drums.

Weston left the circus in Cincinnati, Ohio, in the winter of 1856 and returned to publishing and sales. In 1859, he published one of his mother's most popular books, 'Kate Felton, or a Peep at Realities'. It was in February of that year, a month before his 20th birthday, that Weston finally discovered he had some athletic ability, and his months spent hiking through the countryside, selling his parents' books door-to-door, paid off in a rather unexpected way.

Edward was working at the office of the *New York Herald* where his boss was a very famous name, the American newspaper legend and popular exclamation James Gordon Bennett. One day, a box had been sent from Bennett's home to the *Herald* office in downtown New York City to be forwarded to Washington by the six o'clock train that evening. The box somehow ended up on the wrong wagon, heading back to the Bennett house instead of to the station. When the mistake was discovered, Weston knew it was his responsibility to do something about it. His memoir takes up the story: 'It was then three o'clock; but, taking into consideration the crowded state of the streets, I took it for granted that the wagon in question would not have gone a great distance in an hour. I determined at once to overtake "that wagon" and bring back the "truant box", if I had to chase it to Fort Washington.'

Amid the jeers of his colleagues, who thought his errand was impossible, Weston set off at a run from the *Herald*'s downtown office on Nassau Street and did not stop until he found the wagon, more than five miles up Broadway on the corner of 70th Street, west of Central Park. As he wrote: 'I was so much exhausted, that I could not stand for some moments; but I soon rallied and with the box in my arms, ran back as far as 59th Street. I then got on board a car, and returned to the *Herald* office a few minutes past 5 o'clock. I had accomplished my undertaking, however foolish. It was my first and last "foot-race".'

The box was delivered to the station on time, and Weston hoped never to take part in a "foot-race", or running race, again. Running, like jewellery-making, was not for him, or so Edward thought in the 1860s. By the time he wrote that memoir, in 1862, just three years after his New York mini-marathon, Edward Payson Weston was on his way to becoming famous himself as 'the world's greatest walker', the 'father of pedestrianism'.

And, whatever he thought then, running would come back into his story one day.

IN 1859, WHEN WESTON CHASED through the Manhattan streets after that errant parcel, America was approaching a nightmare. In just two years, northern and southern states would be at war, the existence of the United States would be in jeopardy.

Economic and political differences had been brewing distrust between North and South for years, but in the 1850s a single issue became the focus of their arguments: slavery. While the movement to abolish slavery was gathering force in the North, the South was pushing for slavery to be permitted in new states.

In 1854, the Republican Party was founded with the stated principle of opposition to further expansion of slave-keeping. The South said it would not tolerate a Republican president, so by November 1860, when Republican Abraham Lincoln stood for election against Democrat Stephen A. Douglas, the scene was set for secession and civil war. Edward Payson Weston, with unintended but faultless timing, chose this historic, dramatic moment to launch his new career.

During the presidential campaign, Weston happened to make

a bet with his friend George Eddy that Abe Lincoln would lose the election. But the Southern and Democratic vote had split in three, making Douglas's candidacy hopeless; Weston had picked the wrong horse. The Republicans won, albeit with only 39 per cent of the vote. Lincoln did not carry a single southern state and when the news of his election reached Virginia, the process of secession began. South Carolina, Mississippi, Florida, Alabama, Georgia, Louisiana and Texas all formally seceded from the United States of America. The arrival in the world of a new nation, the Confederate States of America, would be announced on 4 February 1861, a month to the day before the president elect was to be sworn in.

Edward's forfeit for losing the bet was to walk the 478 miles from Boston State House to Capitol Hill, Washington, in ten consecutive days, to attend Lincoln's inauguration. The same event that pitched Americans into a war among themselves was the starting gun for Weston's career as a pedestrian. But if this bet between friends was the start of Weston's life as a professional athlete, he was not aware of it. In his pamphlet 'The Pedestrian' he wrote: 'It was simply a banter between ourselves while dining together one day, and I do not suppose that either of us at that time had the remotest idea of ever attempting such a task. For my own part, I was not aware, at the time, that I possessed any great locomotive powers.' In fact, Weston was about to discover his niche: not only did he excel at long-distance walking, it also turned out to be the perfect sport for a salesman and a show-off.

To start with, though, Edward doubted he could complete the walk and did not finally decide to attempt it until Christmas Day, weeks after the election. On New Year's Day 1861, Weston made a trial of his abilities as a pedestrian, by walking from Hartford to New Haven, Connecticut, a distance of 36 miles. The hike took him 10 hours and 40 minutes, including an hour-long stop for lunch, and he turned this trial walk into a business opportunity. On the road out, he delivered circulars to 150 houses advertising a certain 'literary work', perhaps one of his mother's or father's books. On his return journey he stopped at 125 houses to collect orders and sold, he said, 'several copies' of the book, whatever it was.

On the evidence of this trip, Weston decided that he could manage the walk to Washington without injury. A second walk to New Haven and back, this time delivering 300 leaflets, reassured him and gave an early demonstration of what made Weston a great athlete. He wrote in 'The Pedestrian': 'Some idea may be formed of the condition of the roads, from the fact that when I reached New Haven there were no soles to my boots. It did not affect me in the least; and, after partaking of a hearty supper, I retired at 8 o'clock p.m. and did not wake until 8 o'clock the next morning. I felt as well as usual, and attended church during the day.'

Weston would always have an amazing ability to recover from extreme exertion. In later competitive walks, other men might be faster than Weston but none could match his power of recovery: half an hour's sleep and a bowl of beef broth were enough to put Weston back on the track feeling right as rain.

WESTON'S VENTURE SOON BEGAN to attract the interest of the press. On 31 January 1861, the *New York Times* noted: 'Mr E.P. Weston walked from New Haven to Hartford and back on Friday and Saturday in less than twenty-four hours. The road was covered with ice and slush. He left a pamphlet at each house on the road. He starts from Boston on the 22nd February to walk to Washington in ten days.'

Having decided that he could cope with the physical demands of walking nearly 500 miles, Weston became absorbed with logistics. He would need a coach and horses to carry his companions and his luggage, and there would be accommodation and food to pay for, so in February he went to New York in search of sponsorship. Grover and Baker Sewing Machine Co. paid him $100 to take with him 50,000 of their business cards and 5,000 circulars. He also took circulars on behalf of druggist Frederick V. Rushton, Esq, photographers Messrs J. Gurney and Son, the Rubber Clothing Co. of 201 Broadway, and a Mr Joseph Burnett of Boston. The leaflets were wrapped together and Weston would leave a package at every house he passed on his route from Boston to Washington.

The Rubber Clothing Co. also provided Weston with 'an entire rubber suit of the best quality' for which Edward would be grateful when the weather turned against him during the first half of his journey. A printed timetable (probably complete with adverts for his sponsors) was published ahead of Weston's departure and he arranged accommodation in towns and villages on his route.

The walk, which Weston would later name 'The Great Pedestrian Feat', turned out to be a miniature of his life and career to come. He recorded every detail in 'The Pedestrian' and during those ten days, he is emotional, dandyish and attention-seeking, hopeless with money and possessing a remarkable talent for finding trouble; he meets adversity with an excuse and turns failure into sort-of triumph; he flirts with pretty fans who present him with flags and kisses; every friendly, noisy reception brings a fillip of joy and confidence and every setback or nuisance sends him into 'the darkest kind of blues', out of which he must goad himself again and again.

The first of those setbacks was hot on Weston's heels as he arrived at the steps of the State House in Boston on Friday 22 February 1861, complaining that he was already worn out by the exertion and anxiety of preparing for his journey. Word of Edward's adventure had spread wide enough so that a crowd of well-wishers had gathered to see him off. Unfortunately, not everyone was there to cheer. As Weston climbed from his carriage, he was approached by Constable A.G. Dawes, who told Weston he was pursuing a claim against him for an unpaid debt, and put him under arrest.

Edward responded 'coolly' and asked the officer to talk with him in his carriage; but, as they walked to the carriage another man approached with another claim, this one on behalf of a D.F. Draper. All three men climbed into the coach and Weston explained that he could not repay the money until he returned from Washington. His pursuers insisted and Weston, in characteristically dramatic style, declared that he would take the 'poor debtor's oath', which would have allowed him to pay in instalments, but that he could not pay right then. In the end, the Draper claim was resolved when Weston agreed that his $25 debt could be paid directly by the Grover and Baker Sewing Machine Co. and deducted from his sponsorship. The other party, Bean and

Clayton, agreed to Weston's release so long as he would settle the claim as soon as possible after his return to Boston. Weston was freed but, still in dramatic mode, insisted that Constable Dawes hold him under arrest until they had reached the city limits.

Weston climbed the State House steps at 12.45 p.m., three-quarters of an hour late, and, he wrote, 'was heartily received by his friends, and greeted with three cheers by the crowd' and by 'earnest and repeated calls for a speech'. He chose to save his breath but did take the time to deny he had wagered money on the result of his walk ('but had wagered six half-pints of peanuts that he would keep up to the time'). He also raised a few boos for his creditors and took a moment to metaphorically wrap himself in the US flag, comparing his walk with Lincoln's journey to the White House: 'Abraham Lincoln had been elected by the people, President of these United States, and he believed that he had been elected to walk to Washington to see him inaugurated, and with God's help he would do it.'

At twelve minutes to one, in wintry New England weather, Weston set off at a rapid pace, accompanied by a cheering, shouting crowd of several hundred, and cleared the first five miles out of Boston in 47 minutes.

ON THE FIRST EVENING OF HIS WALK, Weston arrived in the town of Framingham. A mile outside the town, he and his companions were met by a group of drummers who escorted them the rest of the way.

At the Framingham Hotel, Weston was 'most sumptuously entertained', and met his first groupies; or perhaps they were Lincoln's groupies, but Weston benefited all the same. A number of ladies had gathered in the hotel parlour to meet the pedestrian, and 'while preparing to leave, quite a little incident occurred ... A gentleman informed him that a lady present desired to send a kiss to the President. Mr Weston said he had no objections to receiving the kiss, but he could not promise to deliver it to the President. Accordingly, the lady kissed him, and the other ladies present did likewise. He told them that he felt very highly flattered, and, bidding them good-night, left the room.'

Three miles on, en route to Worcester, Massachusetts, Weston was again detained by fans. A carriage stopped containing two ladies who had travelled ten miles to shake his hand. Weston thanked them for their attention and went on his way 'at a brisk pace, and continued to improve mile after mile' despite snow. Passing through the village of Westborough, a 'verdant youth' urged Weston that he must reach Washington on time as the young man had a $20 bet on his success. Weston wrote that 'he promised to do his best, but at the same time expressed his regret, that any one should have bet upon his performance of a feat, such as he had never before attempted'.

Close to midnight, the party ran into trouble. On the approach to Worcester, they met an open carriage 'containing two men; their faces were completely hid as though they were afraid of freezing'. The two men were a sheriff and a Mr Balcom, another of Weston's unhappy creditors, and Weston was again arrested. This time he was not so cool, not surprising given that it was midnight and he had walked many miles. 'The Pedestrian' relates: 'He was so unfit from over-excitement to attend to any matter of business that his friends took the matter in hand.'

There was, however, a happy ending as two men, 'almost entire strangers', offered to act as guarantors for Weston's promise to pay up within two months. Despite this, by the time Weston repaired to 'a friend's house' at two o'clock in the morning, fatigue and stress were starting to tell. He was unable to eat the 'bounteous supper' laid on for him and 'behaved more like a madman than anything else'. All the same, he rested for only an hour, getting back on the road by 3.15 a.m.

The next six miles to Leicester took Weston, for the first time, to the limits of exhaustion. He appeared delirious with lack of sleep, complained that he could not keep his eyes open and could barely stand up. Several times he fell into the deep snow and at one point ordered his companions to turn back to Worcester, then as quickly changed his mind. As Weston wrote: 'He seemed to think that if he went back at all it would be a failure, and if he went ahead it would kill him, yet said that he would sooner die on the road than back down. No one can imagine what a long and tedious walk it was to Leicester through snow nearly two feet deep.'

Long and tedious indeed. Every few minutes, Weston stopped walking to lie down in the snow, and the six miles to Leicester took four hours. With two miles to go, however, his nose started to bleed heavily, which strangely seemed to revive him. By the time he had washed and had eaten doughnuts in Leicester he was fully recovered and ready to continue walking.

At 8.40 a.m. on Saturday 23 February, 19 hours after setting off, the party arrived in East Brookfield, Massachusetts, and Weston finally slept, though only for two hours and with his friends waking him every 15 minutes.

At midday, Weston hit the road once more. From Brookfield he was escorted by a 12-piece brass band; a few miles on at West Warren a lady presented him with a small American flag and a cannon was fired in salute of the walker. When the little flag was attached to the carriage the horse took fright, threatening to overturn the coach. As Weston's diary tells it: '...we were in imminent peril of being capsized, but we soon checked him, and consoled ourselves by thinking he was not the first, neither will he be the last creature, that has trembled at the American flag.'

During the next days of Weston's walk, while he was assailed by snow and rain, he was also buoyed by cheering crowds, by the kindness of people who gave him food and accommodation but refused to take any payment, and by the sight in towns and villages along the road of 'the ever-glorious Stars and Stripes flung to the breeze'. The glory of the Union flag becomes a theme of Weston's memoir: by the end of February, Civil War was just weeks away and the star-spangled banner was in danger of losing at least seven of its stars. If the Union was to survive, it was to be hoped that the rebel states would tremble like spooked horses as Weston predicted.

TO MAKE IT TO WASHINGTON in time to see Lincoln sworn in, Weston had to make around 50 miles per day. By Saturday evening, he was already more than four hours behind schedule. He arrived in Palmer,

Massachusetts, to find a crowd who had been waiting for him since two in the afternoon. There Weston slept for five and a half hours and left the place in the early hours of Sunday morning. Despite, or perhaps because of, having rested, Weston complained of physical discomfort for the first time, with pain in his left knee. At 6 a.m. it started to rain and the walker tried out his rubber suit. Mud made the going slippery and Weston became irritable.

On Sunday evening he reached Hartford, Connecticut, which was where the pedestrian had run up those pesky debts the year before. After meeting with friends and sleeping for three hours, Weston set off again at midnight. Seven miles outside Hartford, Weston was chased by a dog and sprained his left ankle, but carried on for another 10 miles before the rough state of the road made it too painful for him to keep going. An hour's sleep and a cup of coffee at Meriden eased the damage and the party pressed on, but he fell further behind his timetable and was irritated by the return of the pain in his knee and by 'mud and slosh' on the road to New Haven. However, when he left New Haven at 5.15 p.m., Weston was accompanied by 'the largest crowd we had witnessed since our departure from Boston'. In Milford, 11 miles on, there were blazing bonfires and ladies waving handkerchiefs.

The next day, Tuesday 26 February, as Weston crossed the border into New York State he clocked two miles in 19 minutes. An enthusiastic crowd accompanied him for the last mile into Port Chester where he was introduced to several ladies before bidding them goodnight and continuing on to New Rochelle. When he arrived there at 10.30 p.m., he was greeted by more young ladies 'who seemed to pity him exceedingly. The pedestrian thanked them for their sympathy, but expressed himself as being very well, and very sleepy.'

At five o'clock the following morning, Weston left New Rochelle to start what should have been a four-hour walk into New York. The roads were rough and the walker and his team crossed Harlem Bridge before 10 a.m. before arriving at the Metropolitan Hotel on Broadway at 11.30 a.m. (Nearly four years later, on 25 November 1864, the Metropolitan would be one of 13 hotels set on fire by Confederate rebels as part of a plot to create terror in New York.) After breakfast Weston paid visits to two of his sponsors, the photographers J. Gurney and Son and the Grover and Baker Sewing Machine Co. At Gurney's studio he was photographed 'as he then appeared' (presumably a little the worse for wear) and at Grover and Baker's premises on Broadway he 'mounted himself upon a table and took a nap'.

Continuing by ferry to Jersey City, and accompanied by George Eddy, the man who won the bet and set Weston on the road to Washington, EPW and his team arrived in Newark by 7 p.m. A large crowd had gathered and Edward needed the help of the police to keep the crowd from slowing him down.

He rested in the City Hotel in Newark and slept for four hours, leaving at half-past midnight, still in the company of the large crowd. A few hours later, in the small hours of Thursday 28 February, Weston again fell victim to exhaustion. Walking through deep mud had slowed him down and tired him out, and he complained of pain in his chest which he thought was caused by eating mustard in his sandwiches at lunchtime. Just as on his first night on the road, he stopped repeatedly, sitting down to sleep on the ground and threatening to turn back. 'He … was exceedingly irritable, which caused the whole party to have the blues of the darkest kind.' As before, he goaded himself into continuing, throwing the blanket off his shoulders and onto the ground, crying, 'No, I won't go back!' then setting off with renewed energy.

That afternoon Weston slept for two hours at the William's Hotel, New Brunswick, New Jersey, where a crowd surrounded the house. After sleep and dinner, he met with Lloyd's Minstrels, a group of 'blackface minstrels'. One of these was John Hodges, the writer of the song 'Buffalo Gals'. It is possible that Hodges knew the pedestrian as a boy, as he had worked as a clown for the Spalding and Rogers Circus at around the same time Weston joined the circus tour in Canada. Before Weston left the hotel a lady requested a lock of the hero's hair, to which 'Weston made no objections'. However, when a local artist (presumably not a young lady) asked the walker to sit for a photograph, he refused irritably.

By this time, it was clear that the 'great feat' was in danger of failure and again the night was difficult. The party left New Brunswick at 2.15 p.m. followed by a large crowd. The roads were good and in a little over four hours they reached South Brunswick, stopping only to eat before continuing towards Trenton, another 20 miles away. In the dark and on rough roads, Edward's mood deteriorated. He complained of excruciating pain in both ankles but refused to ride in the carriage, instead stopping every few minutes to rest. Seven miles short of Trenton, at a tavern in Clarksville, Weston gave in to exhaustion and agreed that 'it was best for all hands to turn in'. The whole party slept from 11.30 p.m. until 6 a.m., the longest rest they had had since leaving Boston six days earlier.

On waking, he recorded: 'Weston appears greatly improved, and seems more confident of success than ever.' Despite a sprained 'great toe' he walked from Clarksville to Trenton in two hours, arriving at 8.45 a.m. on Friday 1 March. By this time, Weston was 12 hours behind schedule but appeared to be enjoying himself too much to start worrying about whether or not he would get to Washington before Lincoln took the oath.

The owner of the American Hotel in Trenton expressed his regret that Weston had not arrived the evening before as the townspeople had planned a 'grand reception' for the walker. Weston excused himself: '... his being detained at Worcester, Mass., had caused the deviation from his time-table, and came very near preventing his arrival here at all'. No matter that he was only held up for two hours in Worcester; Weston's outrage at his creditors allowed him to blame them for any length of delay.

That morning Weston was greeted by a mysterious stranger: 'Just before the pedestrian sat down to breakfast, and while standing in the bar-room of the Hotel, a gentleman hastily entered, and handing to Mr. Weston a sheet of music, said, he was requested to give it to the pedestrian, and then immediately left the room, giving Mr. Weston no chance to thank him or ask who was the donor.'

The piece of music was called 'Liberty's Reveille' and was dedicated to the Hon. John J. Crittenden of Kentucky. In December 1860, Senator Crittenden had published the Crittenden Compromise, which proposed to write into the constitution a guarantee that slavery could continue in the South. It was one of many unsuccessful attempts to prevent the break-up of the Union. If Weston's story is true and not just an attempt to write himself into history, then the incident illustrates both his growing fame and that his walk was perceived as a political gesture, whatever Weston's personal reasons for walking. Weston was simply looking for an agreeable way to make a living.

Stopping at Philadelphia that night, EPW complained that the flag and brick sidewalks were uncomfortable to walk on. At the Continental Hotel, the best hotel in the city, he was invited to try out the new steam elevator, but chose to take the stairs, noting in his memoir: 'As he commenced to walk he thought he would not alter his mode of travel until he arrived at Washington.'

The party left the hotel at 3.30 a.m., supplied with a new stock of advertisements and heading for Baltimore, Maryland. Twelve miles on, they found out they had taken the wrong road and Weston lost his cool. He 'drank a great quantity of water, and this made him feel quite sick and weak'. A few hours later, after an hour's nap in a private house, Weston, perhaps sickened of water, 'decided to stimulate for the first time on the journey' and drank a small sherry. The sun came out (perhaps also for the first time), the crowd gave him three cheers and on he went.

After a short stop in Hamerton, Pennsylvania, the party set off for Port Deposit. During the 40-mile walk, through the early hours of Sunday 3 March, the 'pedestrian could not find any refreshments to do him good'. Arriving in the Port, the party took the wrong road again and Weston's mood was further darkened, this time by the fact that he walked down the main street in his 'undress uniform' on a Sunday. Furthermore, because it was a Sunday the ferry across the Susquehanna River was not running and the owners had to be found and the boat got ready. It was after 4 p.m. by the time Weston was able to continue his walk. He now had only 21 hours to get to the Capitol but, with a large crowd to watch him, the pedestrian was light-hearted enough to leap a fence nearly as high as his own head. A few miles later the crowd dispersed and he became sleepy and cross again; without an audience to entertain he was left to brood on his fatigue and the probability of failure.

THE FINAL DAY OF WESTON'S WALK TO WASHINGTON, Monday 4 March, started as it meant to go on: 'It was very dark and the clouds were threatening in their appearance. The pedestrian grew weary and almost disheartened ... what with hills, dogs, and darkness, it was a long and tedious journey to Baltimore.' Weston arrived in the city at 4.30 a.m. Maryland was the only 'slave state' and the only Democrat state on Weston's route, though it had not seceded.

Weston left Baltimore at 6 a.m.; he walked fast and grew confident of reaching Washington on time but, seven miles on, disaster struck. Weston had outwalked the horse pulling his companions' carriage, and exhausted it. He walked four miles off his route in search of a replacement, failed to find one and instead told his friends to continue to Washington by train and that he would finish the last 30 miles of his journey alone. 'Mr Weston walked very fast, and hardly stopped while walking the entire distance; indeed, on his arrival at Washington his lips were very much parched. He touched the Capitol as the clock struck 5pm.'

He was four hours too late. In Washington, the weary and disappointed walker met with friends and slept for an hour. He went to the Inauguration Ball but was too sleepy to enjoy it and left at 10.30 p.m. to go to bed. He did not wake until 11 o'clock the next morning.

LATER THAT DAY WESTON WAS INTRODUCED to Members of Congress, including Stephen A. Douglas, the Northern Democrat candidate Weston had backed to win the election in his bet with George Eddy, and who, like Weston, had narrowly missed out. Douglas congratulated Weston on his safe arrival and invited EPW to visit him at home.

On the evening of 7 March, Weston was among those who attended the President's first levee in the Blue Room of the White House. Lincoln spent two hours shaking hands and bending his head to speak to his well-wishers. The new president offered to pay Weston's train fare back to Boston but Weston said that having failed in his first attempt, he would walk back.

DURING HIS FEW DAYS IN WASHINGTON, Weston became infuriated with himself. People kept saying, 'What a shame you missed by just a few hours.' He was convinced that he could do the walk in ten days and he planned to do the journey again in reverse. However, history intervened: with the rebellion making it too dangerous to walk, Edward returned to Boston by train after all.

He made another plan to begin a new attempt on the ten-day walk on 23 April. War began on 12 April and Weston decided it would not be proper for him to waste time on sporting pursuits and that he must put his 'pedestrian abilities' to the service of the government. So it was that he 'prepared to take a WALK IN DISGUISE THROUGH BALTIMORE'.

The story of this little adventure appears as a postscript to 'The Pedestrian'. Weston apparently offered to deliver mail to the Massachusetts and New York regiments stationed at Annapolis and Washington DC. The tale of his journey reads like an odd mixture of boy's own adventure and advertorial, Huck Finn with sponsors to thank. Weston's disguise, that of 'a Susquehanna Raftsman on a bender', was provided by Messrs Brooks Brothers of New York, with a hat supplied by Mr G.W. White of 216 Broadway. He took 117 letters from Boston and New York, sewed into a cloth bag (supplied by the Rubber Clothing Co.) and on 26 April, under cover of night (and carrying an excellent lunch supplied by the Kingsley Hotel, corner of Broadway and Maiden Lane) Weston took a train to Philadelphia and then walked the road he had travelled those few weeks before.

His scrapes are by the book. He sneaks on shaking legs past sleeping sentries and drunken soldiers, gets round suspicious locals by acting dumb. Eventually, the valiant postman ran into the 69th Regiment of New York and was arrested under suspicion of being a Southern spy. Weston spent hours locked up in the guardroom ('a nasty, filthy place') and more hours under guard in the officers' quarters. It was not until the next day that Weston managed to convince his hosts of his true identity ('and when it was known who I was, Colonel Corcoran and his officers insisted that I was their guest and not their prisoner'). Weston was again keeping illustrious company. Just a few months later Colonel Michael Corcoran would be imprisoned and threatened with execution by the Confederates following his capture during the First Battle of Bull Run.

Weston finally attempted the return walk from Washington to Boston in May 1862, but was injured in a fall on a riverbank and seems to have abandoned the attempt after just one day.

CHAPTER

3

CHICAGO:

'IT'S ALL WESTON,

WESTON, WESTON'

WHILE WESTON WAS MAKING HIS SECOND, brief and abortive attempt at the Washington to Boston walk, the Civil War was grinding on with dreadful loss of life on both sides. By the time the last hostilities ended, in the summer of 1865, more than 600,000 men had died either on the battlefield or in military hospitals. Abraham Lincoln was assassinated on 14 April, Good Friday, the same year.

Weston's father Silas, his teenage brother Emmons and his brother-in-law (Charles Delanah, married to Ellen) fought as volunteers. Emmons served with the navy and with the 1st Rhode Island Regiment of Light Artillery. Silas fought with the 3rd Rhode Island Regiment and Charles with the 1st Rhode Island Cavalry. Both men were captured by Confederates and imprisoned at Andersonville, Georgia, where they contracted typhoid. Silas was released and then honourably discharged on doctor's orders in 1863, but Charles died in the prison in April 1864, leaving Ellen alone with a four-year-old daughter.

While the men were away at war, Weston's mother Maria

had moved in with Ellen and the little girl; when Silas returned to Providence, instead of moving into Ellen's house, he boarded nearby and worked as a bookkeeper. The reason for this separation is unclear: it could have been that there was not enough room for Silas in Ellen's house, or perhaps he and Maria no longer wanted to live together. If it was the case that Silas and Maria's relationship had faltered, it would not be the last unhappy marriage in the Weston family.

In 1866 Silas set himself up as a photographer working in a saloon, but died in September of that year. The graves of Charles, Silas and Emmons (who died in an accident in Liverpool, England, in 1865 aged just 19) are side by side in the Weston family plot in Grace Church Cemetery, Providence.

It is not known what Edward Payson Weston did during the Civil War but it seems that he did not fight, though at some time in his life he joined the New York State National Guard. He was not one of the 75,000 volunteers to answer Lincoln's appeal; perhaps he was lucky enough to escape the draft lottery that followed the passing of the Enrollment Act in March 1863. All men between the ages of 20 and 35 were entered into the draw and those whose names were pulled out had to either fight, pay $300 or find a substitute to take their place. Many middle-class men paid their way out of fighting and perhaps Weston was one of them.

After the war was over, Edward published his mother's newest novel, 'Bessie and Raymond; or Incidents Connected with the Civil War in the United States', a morality tale centred on the lives of the women left at home. Weston was by now newly married to Maria Fox and the couple's first daughter, Lillian, was born in Massachusetts on 18

October 1865. She would be followed by Maud two years later and a boy, Ellsworth, two years after that. Weston returned to the *New York Herald*, first as a messenger boy then as a police reporter. According to Joyce Litz's 'The Montana Frontier': 'Weston's speedy walking ability really gave him an edge over reporters from rival papers. He would race to a story on foot and return copy to his editor, in some cases before rival reporters were even on the story's scene.'

The same year Maud was born and not quite a year after his father's death, Weston was in debt again. Having, he said, 'entrusted money to other parties' and lost it all (in who knows what ill-advised speculation), Weston owed thousands of dollars to 'kind friends'. He had tried to repay the money but, he said, barely made a living for his family. At this low point in his family's fortunes, Edward happened to meet businessman George K. Goodwin, who asked if he was still walking. Goodwin was the manager of a circus and menagerie and a fleet of 'moving panoramas' which toured the country. These were the cinema of their day, showing audiences a giant scrolling mural of such dramatic scenes as Civil War battles or life in the Arctic. By the end of their conversation, Weston had taken his first step towards becoming a professional pedestrian.

Edward's family was dismayed, and so was Maria's. Lillian would one day write: 'I don't know if they would have felt much worse had they heard he was a second-story man [a burglar] or a safe breaker; perdition must surely be the goal of such a career.' Lillian said that his choice of career made him the black sheep of the family: 'His respectable relatives didn't understand him; they regretted that he did not embrace a dignified occupation like banking, or selling groceries, insurance or dry goods.

To make a man with my father's erratic disposition lead a humdrum life of that description would be like hitching a racehorse to a plow, or expecting an eagle to act like a barnyard fowl.' Lillian's granddaughter Joyce Litz has written that the family considered pedestrianism 'a low-class profession' and that they never recognised him as the great athlete he was or the acknowledged role he played in developing the sport of pedestrianism. (Weston's mother was not quite so horrified as the others. She made him promise never to walk on sabbath days and was a little reassured; her son was not actually going to the devil, after all.)

Weston, however, was not the man to change his plans to please his family, and anyway he needed money to pay off his debts. So in the late summer of 1867, he took up an extraordinary challenge, to walk more than 1,000 miles in 30 days. This time he found the fame that his attention-seeking nature enjoyed so much.

The horror and chaos of the war were over but reconstruction was proving a messy and difficult business. People were ready for a distraction and Weston's walk fitted the bill. For a short time, his journey became the talk of America. As the New York magazine *Harper's Weekly* had it: 'This walk makes Weston's name a household word, and really gives impetus to the pedestrian mania which has become so general.' But the walk also made him the subject of ridicule, of accusation and vilification, even of death threats.

Just like his walk to Washington, this one began with a bet, this time with $20,000 at stake.

Goodwin bet a fellow businessman, T.F. Wilcox of New York City, $10,000 that Weston would walk the post road from Portland, Maine, to Chicago, Illinois, a distance of 1,226 miles, in 30 consecutive days.

Weston was not to walk on Sundays (as promised to his mother), so he only had 26 walking days to complete the distance. Weston's reward if he succeeded was a purse of $4,000. He would win another $6,000 if he could walk 100 miles in 24 hours at some point along the route. He was allowed five attempts at this extra challenge.

Four witnesses, two for each side, were recruited to accompany Weston: John Grindell, a champion long-distance runner and trainer, and Edward Ingalls, a confidential agent, for Goodwin; and Benjamin M. Curtis and John T. Laphen, described as 'strangers appointed by postmasters', on behalf of Wilcox. The four are described in the articles of agreement of the wager as 'trustworthy and reliable men' whose role was to monitor Weston's progress. The truth of this would later be questioned by journalists who suspected the men took a more active part in the progress of the bet.

In a letter to his four companions, Weston wrote that John Grindell was to 'assume entire charge of my person' with no interference from the others, 'as I rely most implicitly on his kindness of heart, experience, judgement and the interest he has in the successful accomplishment of this race'. Edward was to eat and drink nothing that had not been prepared under Grindell's immediate supervision, according to Goodwin's wishes.

Weston's involvement in the wager (which was worth many times the average annual salary) sparked accusations that he was not an athlete but a 'sporting man', a much less noble breed. EPW defended himself in a letter to the *Providence Journal*. For a man who said he was not religious, Weston often found it convenient all the same to invoke his 'Maker', but he knew how to play to his audience:

Some people condemn me for this undertaking and look upon it the same way as they would upon a prize fight. They think because my Maker has endowed me with perhaps greater walking abilities than most of my fellow men, and because I walk for a wager, no matter to what laudable purpose my winnings will be applied, that I must be classed with prize fighters. Now this is a slander of an honest man who will do anything under the sun that will legitimately enable him to liquidate his debts.

I have never witnessed a prize fight in my life as it is a species of brutality that has ever excited my utter abhorrence. I am not a sporting man in any sense; but a plain business man, and I fail to see wherein I am doing wrong. If baseball or boat racing is a crime, then I am wrong.

At the same time, the 'plain business man' had 30,000 copies of his timetable printed up, along with studio photographs of himself that he would sell on his route along the post road for 25 cents apiece. Weston was never afraid to promote himself or his ventures. He always believed absolutely that his motivation (whether that was the need to pay off his debts or, later, to promote a variety of causes) was honest and laudable, but newspaper editors and journalists soon took a different view.

The photograph shows a small, slight man (at 5 feet 7½ inches, he weighed 125lb) with delicate features and thick, shiny hair, gazing placidly along a painted road. A few years later, when Weston was in his thirties, a reporter from the *New York Herald* described the walker's curiously un-athletic appearance:

The general appearance of the man suggests the presence of nervous rather than physical force. His face is thin, his nose peaked and his chin small and well-rounded. He has a mouth full of energy and dogged determination; he is evidently a person — if he had not bent his whole mind and the undivided force of his character upon the production of bunions, and soft corns, and blood blisters on the alluvial bottoms of his own feet — who would have accomplished some great things in the world.

The *Utica Daily Observer* painted its own picture when he passed through the town 11 days into his walk: 'He is as slim and sinewy as a man can well be made, one of the best specimens of a Yankee under thirty.' Further into the walk, the ladies who 'everywhere seem to take the greatest interest in his success' were 'amazed at the smallness of Weston's feet and hands'.

Weston is photographed smartly dressed, as he always loved to be, and he carries the switch which he used during his walk both to whip life back into his own legs and to shoo troublesome boys from his path. Appearance was important to Weston; he dearly wanted to be seen as a respectable member of America's growing middle class and he adored attention and admiration. He almost always changed into a long coat and gloves before entering a town and would sulk if circumstances forced him to appear in public in 'un-uniform'. Near the end of the walk, he told a reporter he was looking forward to walking into Chicago in his most 'killing' outfit.

Weston's walk from Portland to Chicago may have made him a household name but it also brought him close to disrepute; he was ridiculed in the press and dogged by accusations that he had 'sold' the race. He drew crowds onto the streets of every town he passed through, was feted with fireworks, brass bands and bonfires, but in the newspapers Weston's celebrity was branded 'unwholesome'. He was no war hero, no great leader or prophet, just a novelty whose fame would fade as quickly as a dream, 'leaving the majority of the people in wonderment at what it had really meant, after all' in the words of the *Chicago Tribune*. But for all that he was dismissed as a silly distraction, there was real drama in his journey, as well as the showmanship, and there was extraordinary determination, endurance and athleticism.

Weston left Portland, on time, at midday on Tuesday 29 October 1867; there were no creditors to delay him on this occasion. He walked the first 105 miles in two incident-free days, arriving in Boston on Hallowe'en to be met by an excited crowd. The *Boston Journal* wrote:

> *On the arrival of Weston the crowd had assumed such pro-*
> *portions as to require the services of a squad of police to assist*
> *in keeping the thoroughfare open. The enthusiasm was intense,*
> *and on his way from Charlestown to Boston, Weston repeatedly*
> *raised his hat in acknowledgement of the numerous cheers*
> *which greeted him.*
>
> > *Mr Weston was dressed in a dark blue cloth jacket, with*
> *pants to match, coming to the knee where they were met by red*
> *woolen stockings, his feet being encased in a heavy pair of boots,*

laced to the ankles. His hat was of white marselles, gathered at the top with a small button. He carried in his hand a small switch, which he occasionally was obliged to use vigorously over the heads and shoulders of some too enthusiastic admirers who impeded his progress.

The next day, Ed started his first attempt at 100 miles in 24 hours. He left Dedham, Massachusetts, at midday on Friday 1 November, aiming for a finishing line in Andover, Connecticut. In Pawtucket, according to the Chicago Tribune, 'in the surging crowd that awaited him there he was thrown down and trampled on, and his trainer fared even worse'. In Providence, Weston's home town, 'the crowd was simply immense, the streets through which he was expected to pass being so packed with people that the horse cars could scarcely force a passage'. Thirty-two miles into the trial, despite his accident in Pawtucket, Weston was in good spirits and confident of success. He left Providence, receiving kisses and wreaths from three young women, and walked on until six the next morning. Despite losing their way twice, the party seemed on course to make the 100-mile trial but with 37 miles left to walk and six hours to do it, Weston's trainer Grindell called the attempt off, blaming Edward's condition following his fall in Pawtucket.

The next attempt lasted a little longer. Leaving Hartford, Connecticut, on Tuesday 5 November, Weston planned to walk 100 miles to a point beyond West Stockbridge. This time he was hampered by a snowstorm and made the finish four hours too late. The failure of Weston's second challenge aroused suspicion. The *Boston Journal* opined: 'The idea is very commonly entertained in this city and vicinity that there is something loose about the great pedestrian trip from Portland to Chicago. It has been noticed that Weston's friends have been very active in betting against this hundred miles a day performance.'

The *Providence Evening Press* went further, suggesting that Weston (who had made a point of saying that he was no sporting man) was in league with a former bare-knuckle boxer and gang member turned politician:

> *It is generally believed Weston is in league with one or more parties who have staked large sums of money against his accomplishing the one hundred mile feat, and he will receive more money by failing in it than he would otherwise. One rumor is that John Morrissey has made a bet of $100,000 dollars that Weston would not do it, and that he is to give Weston $20,000 in order that he may win. There are strong evidences that he might have made the one hundred miles either in the first or second trial if he had been so disposed.*

John Morrissey was the elected Congressman for New York, a man whose career had flowered in the corruption and violence that suffused city politics. He used his fists to escape poverty and politics to make his fortune. In the late 1840s, he was hired by the Democrats as muscle, making sure voters found their way to ticking the right box on polling day. He was a member of the pro-Democrat 'Dead Rabbits' gang, the instigators in 1857 of a bloody riot which killed 12 people. He had also been suspected of involvement in the assassination of his Whig counterpart, Bill 'the Butcher' Poole.

Morrissey quickly began to reap the benefits of his political links. Having made some money, and a name, as a prize-fighter and gambler, he opened a betting parlour and his friends in Tammany Hall made sure the police did not interfere. By the 1860s Morrissey owned a string of casinos as well as a stake in a racecourse, and in 1866 stood for Congress.

Whether Weston was involved with Morrissey or not, the mud would soon begin to stick, though not just yet. The *Chicago Tribune* on 12 November still described Weston as a gentleman and a hero. In truth, he was more of an adventurer, happy to take opportunities where he found them. Nonetheless, his company was good enough for a future and a former president, Grover Cleveland and Millard Fillmore, who ate dinner with Weston. And the crowds still turned out. In Rochester on 13 November 'a crowd of several thousand' were hoaxed into following a fake Weston, a wag walking swiftly down the main street in company with a carriage. According to the *Rochester Democrat*, once the young man's deception was discovered he had to run, fleeing from the 'shouting mob'.

The tide turned against Weston, in the papers at least, when he abandoned his third trial, suffering from swollen feet, and with just nine miles to do in three hours. The *Titusville Morning Herald* put Weston on its front page but made enormous fun both of the walker and of his admirers who thought him 'the greatest man the world ever saw', greater far than Washington or Grant. The paper implied that Weston was a drinker, claiming his third 100-mile challenge would have succeeded had he not 'stubbed his toe on a whisky bottle'. The *Herald* was wrong: Weston used lots of whisky and probably smelled powerfully of the stuff but he was not drinking it. He believed that soaking his feet in whisky prevented blisters and throughout his career had a habit of pouring liquor into his boots during walks.

When Weston reached Iowa, the *Davenport Daily Gazette* also made him front-page news, devoting two columns to ridiculing the man, 'the fine art' of pedestrianism and the press and public interest in him. 'Pedestrianism has become a disease,' the *Gazette* lamented. 'Congress meets in a week or so. Nobody talks about Congress. It's all Weston, Weston, the walkist — Weston, the pedestrian. He's the man.'

The paper delightedly pastiched the seriousness with which other newspapers had related details of Weston's life, personality and appearance. The *Gazette* quipped: 'His pedigree is a lively one, and we are informed by a man from Maine, who ought to know, that it reaches clear back. He began to walk quite early. When a year old he achieved the distance from the house to the pig pen, and after that gained every day. He always liked his victuals and walked into them with a regularity and ability that would have been appalling to anyone but a born pedestrian's parents.'

The paper took the attitude that: 'Doubtful things are very uncertain, and Weston is doubtful ... Mr Weston intends ... to put up a bet ... that he can live a hundred years from the first of January. It is understood that several gentlemen of immense wealth who are willing to back him, believe in his ability to do it in a given time.'

The *Cleveland Herald* took the thing more seriously:

> *Weston sets out on his one hundred mile journey, does half*
> *of it with perfect ease, gaining time all the way, and with no*
> *signs of fatigue; makes three fourths of the journey, still ahead*

*of time and not suffering in the least, swings along the last part
of the stretch at the rate of five miles and a half an hour, as
fresh as a lark, and has but nine miles more to go with three
hours and seven minutes to do it in, when he — no, not he,
but the men who have him in charge — declare that he can go
no farther ...*

*It is said ... that the whole thing is a 'put up' that Weston
is hired by his backer and 'opponent' for $4,000 to walk from
Portland to Chicago in 30 days; that between the two points
he is to be wholly under the control of the 'ring' who tell him
when to go and when to stop ... Weston having sold himself
under those conditions considers the whole affair a legitimate
transaction so far as he is concerned, and will live up to his
bargain, although he bitterly feels the degrading fact of his being
made a stool pigeon by the men who have him under control.*

Weston had said himself that he would do 'anything under the sun'
to pay off his debts. In all likelihood, one of these papers was right:
he was taking money from Morrissey, or had been hired by Goodwin
and Wilcox to deliver them the right result. When Weston began his
fourth hundred-mile attempt, from Toledo, Ohio, to Rome City,
Indiana, on 23 November, the story became more serious. According
to the *Chicago Tribune*, Weston was the victim of attempted sabotage. In
a special despatch from Cleveland, the *Tribune* alleged that 'roughs
attempted to jump upon him at Fremont, but were prevented by the
police'. Also during this fourth trial, doubt emerged about the accuracy
of the distances on Weston's route. The distance of each stage had been

provided by postmasters, who according to the Chicago Tribune mis-understood what had been asked of them and provided distance by railroad rather than by turnpike, cutting out the 'turns and twists and angles' and shortening distances by tens of miles. In fact, by the end of the walk, Weston reckoned he had covered closer to 1,300 than 1,200 miles. On the evening of the fourth trial, controversy over how far Edward had actually walked and how much further he had to go caused him to abandon the attempt once more.

The next day was briefly enlivened, according to the *Defiance Democrat* newspaper, by the attentions of a 'good-looking female, prob-ably not more than thirty years of age' and apparently in the grip of Weston-mania, who intruded upon him as he dressed. The woman had knocked at the door of Weston's bedroom a few times and been refused entry, so she bided her time and the next time one of Weston's friends walked into the room, she crowded in and was in the middle of the room before the pedestrian could 'seize a convenient garment to cover himself'. The woman was thrown out, but 'her curiosity gratified ... she went among her friends triumphant'. Weston remarked: 'That woman beats the devil.'

As Weston began his fifth and final attempt (if he failed this one he would forfeit his $6,000 bonus), excitement and anxiety were at their height. On leaving Waterloo City, Indiana, he was joined by a group of men. The *Tribune* reported: 'Just before his departure ... several strangers made their appearance and volunteered their services as an escort to Kendallville; but as they were unknown in these parts, it was not considered safe to accept their offer. One of these men reminded me of a couplet in Byron's Corsair. He was "as mild a mannered man as ever scuttled ship or cut a throat".' The journalist's quote might have been slightly mangled and misattributed (it was from Byron's Don Juan), but his assessment was no doubt accurate.

The correspondent wrote that Weston had promised a friend he would complete the 100 miles on time or die trying, and the writer continued ominously: 'We will see what we will see.' He added: 'The people along the road with whom I have conversed, are filled with the belief that Weston will never be permitted to reach Chicago uninjured. They fear that he will be abducted or poisoned.' Weston began to share those fears and, according to the journalist, arranged for the Chicago police to accompany him on the final 75 miles of his journey. No doubt fatigue exacerbated Weston's anxiety; but equally, if he had involved himself with characters like John Morrissey he may have had reason to be fearful.

In South Bend, the crowd rushed the hotel where Weston rested, some forced their way in, others 'amused themselves outside by breaking the windows and cursing their luck'. Weston chose this place to abandon his final 100-mile attempt. He said the crowd had trampled his left foot and that if he carried on walking he would risk failing to reach Chicago at all. As the *Tribune* writer said: 'I have no comments to make. The readers of *The Tribune* are free to judge for themselves whether the race has been sold or not.'

The same edition of the Tribune carried an editorial calling for sober reflection on the worth of Weston's contribution to mankind: 'Just now the individual who stands on the very peak of publicity; about whose age, height, weight, food, drink, flannel shirt and slightest word and motion, the populace are most intensely interested, and whose steps are followed by gaping throngs, is a not remarkably gifted youth whose greatness is in his legs.' Weston's 'notoriety' was that of the perpetrator of a 'horrible crime' or of a contortionist. 'Let us moderate our ecstasies over novel nothings,' the writer pleaded.

However much the newspaper editors complained, the people of Chicago were not listening. Weston's arrival in the city, on time on Thanksgiving, brought onto the streets such a crowd, 'such a picture of human life as we may scarcely expect to see repeated'.

According to the *Tribune*, anonymous threats on Weston's life prompted Chicago's police superintendent to send a platoon to meet the walker at the city limits. A company of horsemen formed an advance guard clearing the way ahead and 80 policemen on foot formed a window surrounding the pedestrian, moving with him as he walked his last mile.

Here was triumph at last for Weston. His failure to meet the 100-mile challenge meant little compared to the adulation of the crowd. The pavements were blockaded, the streets choked with buggies, handkerchiefs waved from every window, balcony, tree and even telegraph pole as the people of the city fought for a view of this man 'not distinguished above his fellow-men by any peculiar quality save that of physical endurance'. As the sound of the Western Light Guard band announced the walker's approach, the fluttering handkerchiefs rolled down Wabash Avenue like 'the white crest of a mighty wave'. By the time the procession neared Weston's finish line at Sherman House Hotel, the people had blocked the streets completely and the police platoon was unable to continue.

Edward was in his element. Mounting the steps of Sherman

House, he kissed his wife and baby, lifting little Lillian into the air for the crowd to admire. The people cheered 'for the good parent, the devoted husband, and also for the pretty baby'. Once Weston had retired to a room in the Opera House, the place was besieged by 'Weston hunters of the gentler sex' who surged up the stairs and 'flattened their fair noses against the glass doors'. Weston, with a 'complacently triumphant smile ... could scarcely refrain from executing a few jubilant capers through the room by way of testifying his joy at being the lion of the day'.

The furore in the street lasted only as long as Weston stayed in the Opera House window. When he went off to eat lunch the crowd melted away. As the Tribune had it, the people 'vanished like a dream, and everyone who had participated in the popular excitement appeared as if suddenly disenchanted and half ashamed of the fever which has smitten them'.

CHAPTER 4

A GENTLEMAN

OF CULTURE

IN 25 DAYS ON THE ROAD TO CHICAGO, Weston had walked an average of 52 miles a day, and though he never completed 100 miles in 24 hours, on three days he covered 91 miles, 80 miles and 70 miles on rough roads, sometimes knee-deep in mud and through rain and fog.

That Thanksgiving afternoon, a couple of hours after his arrival, Weston was booked to speak at the city's Opera House. His main concern was to use this public appearance to undo the damage he felt his name and reputation had suffered in the last few weeks. He was introduced to the audience by a Mr J.W. Sheehan as 'America's great "walkist"': 'Mr Edward Weston is known to you, and to the country generally, as an athlete in the particular line in which he has just finished his performance, but to his friends and acquaintances, he is also known as a journalist and editor and consequently a gentleman of culture and respectability.'

When he addressed the audience himself, Weston spoke about the mental and emotional strain he had undergone. He said he had been 'under a great state of excitement during the whole time', continuing: 'I have been obliged to strain my nervous system to the utmost in order to accomplish this task, and have hardly known what I have been about some of the time.' He reiterated the claim that his life had been in danger: 'I received numerous anonymous letters – letters, written, no doubt, by parties who had wagered against me, in which I was threatened and it was stated that I would not come into this city alive.'

Later in the speech, Weston showed his political skill, jumping on a couple of bandwagons. For the first time, he aired his thoughts on pedestrianism, saying: 'Walking as an exercise is something I wish to see encouraged – something that I think will benefit the youth of America – will benefit the youth of any land. It is an exercise, not only healthy, but it is a pleasure, at times, and as good an exercise as a man can take.' There was a fair amount of hand-wringing going on in the later half of the 19th century about the effect that the arrival of mass passenger transport might have on the health of the population. Aside from the worry that people would become lazy and unfit, the new trains and streetcars were not terribly safe for either passengers or staff, as the private companies that ran public transport tended to put profit before safety. The same had been true of the old steamboats, like the one Weston had worked on as a boy, which had a tendency to explode.

Weston finished his speech with a bit of grandstanding, sounding another note he knew would be popular:

> I don't contend that I have done anything more than any American young man can do. But I must contend it is with pride I do say, that I think it would puzzle an Englishman to do it ... I don't propose to join the sporting fraternity, but I do

propose, so long as I can stand on two feet, if any Englishman

gets up and walks from Portland, Maine, to Chicago, Illinois,

… better than I have, I shall think it my bounden duty, out of

respect to the plaudits that I have received from the American

people, to get up and beat him.

In 1867, when Weston made his speech, England was no longer the United States' owner or its enemy, but had become a favourite rival. The US was expanding and industrialising rapidly: Nebraska had become the 37th US state in March, and in the same year Alaska was purchased from the Russians; railroads carried goods and people from coast to coast, while great waves of immigration kept the population growing rapidly, helping to exploit the vast land and its resources. America was on its way to becoming the world's greatest industrial nation; if in the meantime it wanted to put little England in its place, Edward was volunteering to help, though it would be a few years before he made good on his promise.

Meanwhile, controversy over Weston's motives rumbled on. On 1 December the *Chicago Tribune* published a letter from the pedestrian refuting suggestions that he had been paid for his appearances at the Opera House and that the walk itself was no more than a 'shrewdly managed "show speculation"'. Newspapers had suggested that Weston had made more than $4,000 from the sale of photographs and time-tables along the route, but in the letter he claims to have made no more than $1,000.

The publicity won Weston a charismatic new cheerleader. On 5 December the *Tribune* published a letter from Dan Rice, 'showman and presidential candidate'. Rice wrote that he and his family had met Weston near Silver Creek, Ohio, during Ed's third attempt at 100 miles in 24 hours. That night, he wrote, there was a 'storm almost as violent as any I have ever, in my long experience, encountered upon the road'. Driving home from Erie to Girard, 'the wind ... blew so tremendously that the ladies were greatly alarmed and apprehensive that the carriage would be overturned ... hurricane kept possession of the night, and even until the next evening the wind was so high as to very seriously retard fast walking, and spiteful snow squalls contributed their cold and wet quota of elementary opposition. Both nights too were very dark, and the lanterns carried by Weston's attendant walkers scarcely dispelled the gloom sufficiently to insure safe footing.'

Rice says that the next morning he expected to hear that Weston had abandoned the attempt. 'Judge then of my astonishment when I learned the next morning that he had successfully battled through that long tempestuous night and was untiringly striding on to apparent victory.' Weston gave up the attempt after 91 miles but this was a far greater achievement, Rice wrote, than to walk 100 miles in fair weather. Rice praised Weston's pluck and his 'wonderful powers of endurance' and announced: 'As an evidence that I deem him both honest and able to do even better than the conditions of his match required, I will wager $50,000, $10,000 to go to Weston if he wins, and the balance to be donated by the winner to any public charity, that he can walk one hundred miles in 23 hours.'

This was an intervention from one of the most famous men in the country, but an ambiguous one if Weston was serious about his reputation. Dan Rice was an extraordinary character, who has been all but forgotten now, as his biographer David Carlyon has pointed out, dubbing him 'the most famous man you've never heard of'. Born illegitimately in New York in 1823, Rice was raised by his mother and stepfather on a series of farms in Manhattan, first on Bowery, then on Fifth Avenue at 14th Street and later on 26th Street, the family edging further and further uptown every few years with the city nipping their heels. Dan's mother died a few days after the boy's 13th birthday and the following year, during the financial 'panic' of 1837, he left home and walked to Pittsburgh where he found work in a stable. He worked as a dray driver, using the horsemanship he had learned from his stepfather. From there, he somehow ended up touring the States with a sideshow, 'Sybil, the Learned Pig'. From this beginning Rice eventually made a fortune as America's most famous clown, a 'talking' clown whose business was not juggling and custard pies, but wit and song, something closer to modern stand-up than anything seen in a circus today. He worked for Henry Spalding, who had co-owned the circus company that Weston toured with in his teens, and in the 1860s he was said to earn as much as $25,000 a year, the same as President Lincoln's salary.

Rice was a dreamer, given to embellishment and exaggeration, and he made his dreams the currency of his job, spinning tall tales into wild fancies to captivate his audience. Circuses were interactive, heckling and audience participation were part of the show, and Rice's great skill was his ability to respond to his audience. Weston too loved to engage his spectators; his spirits would rally to the sound of cheering and it was in the loneliness of country roads when the crowds were left behind that he lost his good humour. Maybe Rice saw something of himself in the younger man, in his itinerant youth, his showmanship and his preference to do anything, take any wager, rather than do an ordinary job. That autumn, Rice had decided to run for president (though he would drop out of the race in February 1868) and he faced the same ambivalent press as Weston: he was either an honest man of the people or a shameful laughing stock, a clown running for president. The very same issue of the Davenport Daily Gazette which had so much fun with Weston at the start of his walk to Chicago summed up its thoughts on Dan Rice in a way that illustrated exactly why Rice was and was not a perfect match for Weston: 'Dan Rice the ex-clown has an organ, which says, "Dan Rice clubs are being formed in different parts of the country, in view of presenting the distinguished equestrian as a candidate for the next President of the United States." Add John Morrissey for Vice President and the ticket will be complete.' In other words, Dan Rice was no better than John Morrissey, with whom Weston had already been linked. Perhaps, then, it is not surprising that Weston did not take up Dan's proposal right away: nothing more was heard of their partnership until autumn of the following year.

WESTON'S LONG WALKS TO WASHINGTON AND CHICAGO, even while the newspapers were calling him 'doubtful', had created an audience for pedestrianism and at the same time opened the door for competitors. By the beginning of 1868, Weston was regularly taking part in pedestrian challenges against the clock or, increasingly, against opponents as pedestrianism grew in popularity. As well as road-walking, he took part in track races. During that year he lost as many bets and races as he won and he was followed by the familiar mixture of suspicion and hyperbole. In April, he finally made 100 miles in 24 hours. In fact, he walked 103 miles and finished with two minutes to spare in spite of walking through snow and mud. In June, at Boston's Riverside Park, Weston attempted 100 miles in 23 hours, in front of a crowd of spectators. He made the first mile in 15 minutes, walking half of it backwards, but made only 90 miles in 22 hours and 52 minutes, reportedly losing a $4,000 purse by his failure to make 100 miles in time.

On 19 June, Weston walked for the first time against George Topley, an English champion pedestrian, at Mystic Park, Boston. Topley completed the first 25 miles ahead of Weston, winning himself $1,000. The match finished after 24 hours when Weston stopped, having walked 75 miles. According to the *New York Times*, Weston was two miles ahead of Topley, who continued walking but stopped to rest at 74 miles and never returned to the track. Soon after, it was announced that Topley had withdrawn from the race and Weston was declared the winner. He had won his first race against England, although it was not the transparent victory he might have wanted.

A month later, another failure. Weston was reported to have tried and failed to complete 50 miles in 11 hours at Forest City Park, Portland. Then in August he met his first regular opponent, a man called Cornelius Payne, from Albany, New York. The 100-mile race took place on a half-mile circular track in Troy, Michigan; 1,500 people paid 20 cents each to watch Weston and Payne compete but the match was capsized by a glass of sherry. Weston had drunk one small glassful (whereas Payne was reported to have taken unspecified 'stimulants' through the night, apparently to help treat diarrhoea) and was undone by giddiness and headaches. Weston was a lifelong advocate for his own version of temperance, which meant moderate consumption rather than total abstinence. In practice, he rarely drank during races while some of his competitors might subsist on a diet of champagne and oysters.

The Utica Observer described the race as a 'fizzle', and suggested that Weston threw the match. EPW walked well for the first 61 miles, which he completed in 14 hours. 'Judging from the time in which he had performed the 61 miles, the other 39 ought to have been play to him, for he would hardly have to average four miles an hour. But from that time forward, he, as it were, "fizzled", made no time at all and allowed Payne to beat him.' But the *Troy Times* called this 'uncharitable': 'We happen to know from the most indubitable evidence that he was sick and not intoxicated, as many people were led to believe from the manner in which he staggered about.' In the end Weston walked 71 miles in 23 hours and 37 minutes and Payne walked 84 miles in 24 hours and 15 minutes. Both men, however, took a share of the $300 received at the gate.

After losing a rematch against Payne in September, Weston complained that he could not walk on circular tracks. He went some way to proving this on 8 October 1868, when he set a world record by walking 100 miles in 22 hours, 19 minutes and 8 seconds. The route, instead of a circular track, was on the roads of New York State and ended in White Plains. The record was never properly ratified but it appeared to serve a purpose. When he broke the record, Weston also passed a test set for him by Dan Rice. On 20 October, Rice wrote a letter published in *Turf, Field and Farm*, a sporting paper which described itself as 'ably edited, independent and fearless' and covering 'a wide range of manly pastimes'. This time Rice made Weston an offer he could not refuse, 'in accordance with the promises I voluntarily gave you, based upon the condition precedent of your successfully performing the feat at White Plains'. The letter continued:

> *If you will walk 5,000 miles, as you propose, in one hundred consecutive days ... I hereby bind myself to secure to you by general contribution, a purse of not less than $20,000. In making the above proposition I am governed by two motives — first, to be the humble instrumentality of rewarding you for a display of physical and moral courage in the face of almost insurmountable obstacles and most cruel and undeserved suspicions and criticism, secondly to foster and encourage a taste for pedestrianism, made requisite by the fashionable and enervating indolence of the times.*

A purse of $20,000 would make a nice prize now, but in 1868 it was the kind of money that would allow Weston never to walk or work again if he chose. A New York garment worker in the middle of the century might make $10 or $20 a week; during the Civil War, Union soldiers earned just $13 per month. To win this life-changing prize, Weston would walk west from Bangor, Maine, through the wild north of New England and around the Great Lakes all the way to St Paul, Minnesota. He would then turn south and walk through Iowa and Missouri as far as St Louis, then head north and east to New York, and as usual, for his mother's sake (Weston himself seemed to tend towards agnosticism for most of his life), he was not to walk on Sundays. He would not be allowed to enter any vehicle at any time except ferries where necessary, and he was to bear all expenses himself. The proposed route would take him through 17 states and more than 700 towns and cities, including Chicago, Cincinnati, Indianapolis, Pittsburgh, Baltimore and Philadelphia. The walk was to begin in December: another winter trek through snow, rain and mud.

WESTON SET OFF, A FEW WEEKS LATER THAN PLANNED, on 19 January 1869. The *Ohio Democrat* gave a flavour of the optimistic and jolly start to Weston's long journey:

> *He started from the steps of the Court House at exactly 4 p.m. An immense crowd lined the streets, and vigorously cheered him on his way. He was dressed in a semi-military costume and flourished a tiny whip in his gloved hand. He started off with a light, springy step, in good humor, and merrily laughing at the quizzing endearments of the ladies, who waved their handkerchiefs at him from the windows of their residences. At 4 o'clock precisely he was kissed by an enthusiastic female admirer. In nine more minutes he had accomplished his first mile, and within an hour he was six miles west of the city, walking as swift and as light as a rabbit.*
>
> *Two close covered carriages accompanied him, containing your correspondent and Weston's backers, with several of his personal friends. The horses are kept at a brisk trot by Weston's feet. At 7 p.m. Weston ate a light lunch without stopping, and*

*as I write, the cheering fragrance of his prime cigar is floating
on the chill breeze behind him.*

Following that blithe start, the first few weeks of his walk were a
hard slog. His route took him through Vermont's Green Mountains,
where the condition of the roads cost him energy and time. He lost
six pounds in weight and days from his schedule. The *Cleveland Courier*
reported: 'It requires no little credulity to believe that he has thus
far walked in mid-winter through Maine and New Hampshire, over
the Green Mountains and through the northern wilds of this state
contending against most discouraging obstacles. He has waded for miles
in snow up to his waist. One day he walked fifty miles without meeting
a team, his party breaking the road. Another day, the most strenuous
exertions only availed to accomplish twelve miles in nine hours.'

Despite the weather, Weston was even more elaborately and
distinctively dressed than usual, in 'a more gorgeous suit than has
been his wont, it being a naval suit, similar to those worn by marine
corps officers, with shoulder knots, and a forage cap of beaver richly
ornamented with bullion and surmounted by a white cockade'. Dressing
so flamboyantly made him easy to imitate and a pair of mischievous
students had fun stealing Weston's thunder in snowy Vermont. In
Burlington, on the evening of Saturday 30 January, a young man in
military uniform passed through the town followed by three horse-
drawn sleighs. He was greeted by the mayor, bonfires were lit in his
honour and a group took part of the road with him. The next morning,
another Weston arrived, the real one this time, two days behind
schedule. The mayor was indignant and a young lady 'who followed the

sham Weston 22 miles in a cutter [sleigh] for the purpose of presenting him with a pair of woollen gloves of her own manufacture' was mortified. The pair tried the same trick in St Albans, Vermont, and were mobbed: '[The sham Weston] ran into the woods in terror while his comrade in the sleigh drove fiercely in the direction of Alburgh.'

Leaving Buffalo for Cleveland on 24 February, five weeks into his trek and having walked more than 1,100 miles through snowy country, Weston was ten days behind schedule. Still, he was confident of success, believing that the hardest part of the journey was behind him and that the western roads would be easier going. Then, suddenly, Weston abandoned the attempt, claiming that he had run out of funds to pay his expenses: another quixotic failure.

There were two more failures awaiting Weston that spring. The second demonstrated how hard Weston was pushing himself. Nearly 90 miles into a race against Cornelius Payne over 100 miles in 22½ hours, Weston was leading the younger man by seven minutes when he collapsed with chest pain.

CHAPTER

HUMBUG!

BY THE END OF THE 1860S, Weston's triumphant arrival in Chicago in December 1867 seemed like a distant memory, blotted out by his numerous failures against Cornelius Payne and his unsuccessful attempt to walk 5,000 miles in 100 days for Dan Rice's $20,000. In the last months of the decade Weston's reputation sank as the press declared that he was a fraud, just as they had long suspected, or at least claimed to have suspected.

This was perhaps not surprising, given the turn his career took during the summer and autumn of 1869, the year his son Ellsworth was born. While still also working as a journalist, he left his wife and young children at home in New York and travelled west to Iowa and north to Wisconsin to perform in a series of 'trials' which was really a season of shows. The *Chicago Tribune* of 27 June 1869 had announced Weston's tour: 'He has concluded a contract with Mr J.T. Landman of London, the conditions of which are as follows. Weston is to walk 50 miles within ten and one half consecutive hours, on thirty different occasions between July 1 and November 1. During each trial, he is to walk one half mile backward. If successful he is to receive $250 for each success, but failing to walk the half mile backward within the given time he is to receive $200.'

An advertisement in the *Dubuque Daily Herald* made plain the character of Ed's new venture: 'Edward Payson Weston, The Great American Champion and Pedestrian of the World, will undertake the stupendous feat of walking 50 miles in 10 1/2 hours, including the most difficult task (in fact against nature) of walking one half mile backward.' Appearing day after day on provincial showgrounds like Dubuque Driving Park must have reminded Weston of his days with the circus. The announcement read like a circus handbill too and his backward walking trick ('against nature'!) clinched it; Weston was an attraction, more strongman than athlete, more sideshow than sportsman. He even had a stage name, 'The Great American Champion'.

As usual, he won some and failed some. In Fort Wayne, Indiana and in Dubuque, Iowa, he earned his $250. Three days after Dubuque, he failed by 90 minutes in Davenport, Iowa, three days after that there was another miss in Joliet, Illinois. And so it went on. The press was quick to brand Weston a 'humbug', a fraud and a self-publicist. That June issue of the *Chicago Tribune* as well as announcing Weston's tour had claimed that he had revealed, 'to a trusting reporter of the *New York Sun*', an extraordinary plan to make another long walk that winter:

> He 'proposes' to make another attempt to walk 5,000 miles in
> 100 consecutive days, his route laying across the continent, and
> San Francisco being the objective point. It is not stated whether
> he is to be allowed extra time in which to recuperate after having

undergone the pleasant process of scalping ... we warn Edward

that photographs of his elegant little self won't sell well among the

Apaches along the route, and that the trip won't pay ... Weston is

a humbug and is beginning to be appreciated as such.

It is not hard to see where Weston got the idea. Just a few weeks earlier, after ten years blasting and building work, the Central Pacific and the Union Pacific Railroads had met in Utah so that finally it was possible to travel by train from coast to coast. Weston was perhaps either inspired or challenged by the new railroad; what a machine could do, so could a man. But for the press this was a step too far. And, in fairness, Weston's proposal must have seemed either unhinged or disingenuous.

The journey across the continent by wagon was still a tough, even dangerous undertaking. During the late 1860s, attempts to confine Native Americans to reserves had failed and around 2,000 Apaches and other braves were roaming the West attacking soldiers, settlers and wagons. There was the weather and the terrain to consider, too. Thirty years later, when Weston's daughter Lillian travelled west from New York to join her husband on their new Montana homestead, she and her tiny children, the youngest just a baby, travelled the last 100 miles by stagecoach. Her three-year-old daughter Barbara was tied to her seat to keep her from tumbling out of the coach as the horses toiled through blizzards and sleet on a road that was little better than a stream bed. Weston was talking about crossing the same country on foot, and in winter; he must have sounded like, well, like a humbug.

This was quite an insult, and one that Weston was not going to put up with for long. A 'humbug' was the newspapers' term for a self-publicist, with dishonesty, exaggeration and lack of substance implied. The most famous humbug, the so-called Prince of Humbug, was P.T. Barnum. Barnum drew visitors to his museum with attractions like General Tom Thumb and the Feejee Mermaid, which were both well known to be fakes but no less fascinating for all that. As Barnum said: 'The public appears disposed to be amused even when they are conscious of being deceived.'

Of course, while newspapers were quick to pounce on humbugs, their own pages were full of dishonest advertising. When Weston was on his walk to Chicago, the same newspapers that so gleefully ridiculed the 'walkist' carried adverts for a variety of patented potions with extravagant powers. One such, Mother Bailey's Quieting Syrup for children, allayed all pain, made sick and weak children strong and healthy, never failed to regulate the bowels and gave mothers rest day and night, all for just 25 cents per large bottle. On the same page of the *Utica Daily Observer* where Weston was denounced as a 'fizzle', Mother Bailey's miraculous preparation appeared three times alongside notices for Doctor Langley's Root and Herb Bitters and The Great Pin Worm Remedy, 'purely vegetable and guaranteed to cure'.

Lying and exaggeration were part of American life, a way of getting ahead in a competitive society. Every show or circus was advertised as remarkable, astounding and amazing. When the West was settled, 'boosters' used white lies to attract railways and settlers to their corner of the prairie, and had their embroideries worked into the map of the USA. At the same time, politics was lousy with corruption. President Ulysses Grant's own brother was implicated in misadministration of supplies destined for Indian reservations. The 'spoils system' allowed Senators and Congressmen to dish out government jobs among their friends, family and supporters.

To our eyes Weston may look like a tiny fish in a big, murky pond but the newspapers did not see it that way. For his part, Weston hated to be the subject of doubt or ridicule; his vanity could not stand this attack on his reputation and during 1870 he fought back. No more was said of walking to California and instead he set about proving once and for all that he was an outstanding athlete and that everything else, the frilly shirts and the antics, was no more than a distraction. During the following months he pushed himself to walk faster and faster: 100 miles in 24 hours was old news, as Weston nudged the clock back to 22 hours and below. And he hit on something else that helped him gain a little respectability and credibility at the same time as winning more attention.

IN APRIL 1870, WESTON TOOK THE ARGUMENT TO NEW YORK, the home of those newspapers that had been most critical. There his path crossed with that of yet another of the most prominent men in the United States, a man only slightly less famous than President Lincoln.

Horace Greeley was one of the great figures of American newspapers and of American history. Along with James Gordon Bennett, who had unwittingly discovered the walker in Weston with his mis-sent parcel, Greeley dominated the New York press during the middle years of the nineteenth century. The child of poor New England farmers, Horace arrived in New York in 1831 in possession of a few dollars and the skills he had learned as a printshop apprentice. He found work on the *Evening Post* and the *Daily Whig* and soon set up his own printshop with a partner, Francis Story. In 1841, Greeley borrowed $1,000 and mortgaged the shop for a further $3,000. On 10 April, he published the first issue of the New York Tribune; after two months the new penny paper's circulation was 11,000. The following September, Greeley launched a weekly edition of the *Tribune* which was amazingly popular, eventually reaching 200,000 Americans.

Greeley was an idealist, and he used his papers to campaign for social justice, believing that his nation's great natural wealth ought to afford a good life for Americans of every class. He was an influential and active member of the Whigs, and then of the Republicans, although his own opinions and those expressed in the Tribune often strayed a long way from the party line. For example, during the 1850s, Karl Marx was a regular *Tribune* contributor.

In the 1860s the paper campaigned for the emancipation of slaves and in August 1862 Greeley published a very famous open letter to President Lincoln, more than 2,000 words long and titled 'The Prayer of 20 Million'. He accused Lincoln of capitulating to the South over slavery by failing to enforce the Confiscation Act, which deemed slaves to be 'spoils of war' and should have been used by the Unionist army to free the slaves of conquered rebels. Greeley said that Lincoln was trying to bribe the South to play nicely with the North by letting it keep its slaves, and furthermore Greeley argued that the Unionists could not hope to win the Civil War without help from black 'scouts, guides, spies, cookers, teamsters, diggers and choppers'. Lincoln replied in a letter printed in the *National Intelligencer*, in which he argued that the issues of

Union and slavery were separate and that if he could win the war without freeing a single slave he would, or if he could win by freeing all slaves he would do that too. However, when a few weeks later Lincoln announced the Emancipation Proclamation, Tribune readers believed this to be at least partly Greeley's triumph.

The Hon. Horace Greeley it was who introduced 'his young friend' Edward Payson Weston to an audience at the Steinway Hall on East 14th Street on 27 April 1870. Weston delivered an hour-long lecture about athletic exercise, then walked a mile inside the 2,000-seat auditorium, just over 17 laps round and round the audience. In a black velvet suit and striped hat, Weston made an extraordinary sight that evening at the Steinway Hall, charging around the rows of seats. The *New York Sun* gave a lively description of the evening's spectacle:

> *The human velocipede was off. He went around the room like a high-pressure steam man. 'Once,' shouted the Hon. Mr Greeley as the pedestrian completed his first circuit of the room. The ladies became excited and sprang upon the seats to get a look at him but he passed like a streak of lightning ... Down, across, and back, the lithe pedestrian went like a hawk on the wing. Snap went his whip about his legs as his calves became numb. On his seventeenth circuit, he snatched a glass of ice-water from the end of the platform, swallowing it at one gulp without diminishing his rate of speed, and tossing the tumbler among Mr Greeley's feet ... As the handsome athlete made his last round the Hon. Mr Greeley, whose eager countenance indicated intense interest, raised his left hand, saying, 'There, there! Stop,*

stop! You've done it' ... Mr Weston had made his mile in exactly
nine minutes and thirty seconds.

By the time of this performance, Greeley had lost control of the *Tribune* but was more than ever involved in politics. Two years later, at the age of 61, he ran for president. Greeley lost to the incumbent President Ulysses Grant but ended his race with a unique place in American history as the only candidate to die before the votes were counted. By then, he and Weston had become good friends, and the young pedestrian was reported to have been at Greeley's side when he died.

A month after his Steinway Hall exhibition, Weston attempted an 'unparalleled task'. He pushed himself further than ever before, attempting 100 miles in 22 hours, a chance to prove in front of an audience and in controlled conditions that he could do much more than just talk about walking. The *New York Times* wrote: 'In consequence of the belief which prevailed among certain classes of people that Weston was a humbug, Mr W. W. Wallace, the enterprising proprietor of the Empire Skating Rink, determined to give New Yorkers an opportunity of judging for themselves.' Weston, or perhaps it was Wallace, decided to invite closer scrutiny of this race, bringing in the City Surveyor to help lay and measure a track, 735 feet 5 inches 'according to official measurement'. Weston would need to walk 717 laps of the Third Avenue Rink, plus an extra 706 feet. A panel of seven judges, New York lawyers, accountants and medics, would monitor Weston's progress over the 22 hours.

At quarter past midnight on 25 May 1870, in front of the judges and just a handful of spectators, the attempt began. Weston completed the first mile in 11 minutes and 55 seconds and the next one ten seconds quicker, 'in splendid condition and excellent spirits' and with 'an easy swinging gait'. By 1 a.m. he had completed 26 laps and, according to the *New York Times*, 'seemed quite confident of the result, and expressed his determination to accomplish his task or die in the attempt'.

Stopping every ten miles or so and snacking on beef tea, crackers, raw eggs and lemonade, Weston crossed the halfway mark at 11 o'clock in the morning, having rested for no more than ten minutes at a time. Having begun his walk in front of the seven judges and a very few spectators, he finished it at 9.45 p.m. 'amid the plaudits of 5,000 persons', in 21 hours and 38 minutes, more than 20 minutes clear. The *Times* wrote: 'He accomplished the 100 miles without giving evidences of any great strain on his mental or physical system, being quite as fresh at the finish as he was at the opening.' Weston had not just won over the crowd, the newspapers too had changed their tune. The *New York Times* again: 'He exhibited good courage and fortitude throughout the long and weary tramp, and was rewarded with the encouraging acclamations of his numerous admirers ... His pedestrian triumph was pronounced to be the finest on record.' The *New York Herald* wrote that Weston 'addressed the crowd from the judges' stand, saying that it was love, not money, which had induced him to attempt the feat which he had just accomplished. It was the desire to free himself from the reputation which had been given to him by some of the daily papers of this city of being a "humbug" and to set right before the public those who had befriended and defended him.'

Weston was no longer complaining that he could not walk in circles as he had after losing to Cornelius Payne in 1868. In fact, walking in an arena or rink suited him well; his worst moments of doubt and despair on road races always hit him on the lonely stretches of road, far from the cheering crowds, whereas on a track he never walked away from his audience. It would be a long while before he tackled another road race. A few days later, on 2 June, Weston capitalized on his success at the Empire Rink by making a 'benefit' appearance. He walked 50 miles with a target time of ten hours, including one half-mile backwards which he completed in 10 minutes and 37 seconds. In velvet coat, kid gloves and hat, in front of a large and reportedly 'very respectable' crowd, Weston finished the walk with nine minutes and 59 seconds to spare, according to the City Surveyor. Horace Greeley timed him in at ten hours and one minute. Regardless of ambiguity, the *New York Times* said: 'Mr Weston will realise about $1,000 by this feat, besides a reputation which will assist him materially in the future.'

WESTON'S TRIUMPH AT THE EMPIRE SKATING RINK was a turning point. He was finally being taken seriously, able to attract a 'respectable' New York crowd. Involving the City Surveyor and a panel of judges picked from the city's professional class had done the trick wonderfully. Now, Weston or his backers decided to take this tactic a little further. EPW approached a group of New York's most prominent doctors, proposing to tackle a walk of 400 miles in five days, including walking 112 miles in 24 hours, and to 'submit himself to more critical scientific investigation' during the walk and for five days before and after. This new 'unparalleled feat' would take place in November, again at the Empire

Rink, 'for the benefit of science and a purse of $5,000'. The track that Weston was to walk on was again the subject of scrutiny. City Surveyor Joseph L.T. Smith gave a written certificate to the effect that once around the track was 735 feet and 84.1 inches; that to walk to 100 miles Weston must walk 717 laps plus 402 feet and 72.1 inches; 803 laps for 112 miles. The whole 400 miles would require Weston to walk the rink 2,870 times plus 139 feet and 2.1 inches over. The measurements were taken along the centre of the track and the survey was witnessed by 50 people.

The 'committee of medical men' included some of New York's most prominent doctors. R. Ogden Doremus was a professor, at different times, of chemistry, physics and pharmacy. During a two-year sojourn in France, where he worked on compressing gunpowder, he met Napoleon III. His work in forensic toxicology brought him to the attention of the press, particularly in a number of cases that involved him performing tests in court to prove that husbands had been poisoning wives. William A. Hammond was a neurologist and had been the Surgeon General of the US Army. In that post he founded the National Museum of Health and Medicine (then the Army Medical Museum), was court-martialed in 1864 after refusing to accept a transfer, but then exonerated by Congress in 1878. He was a co-founder of the American Neurological Association and has both a disease and a species of toad named after him. Austin Flint co-founded Buffalo Medical College in 1847 and was a professor at Bellevue Hospital Medical College. He held the presidency of both the New York Academy of Medicine and the American Medical Association. William H. Van Buren was chair of anatomy at the University of the City of New York and a professor at Bellevue

Hospital Medical College, as well as vice-president of the New York Academy of Medicine.

Everything Weston ate during the walk was to be weighed and measured by these illustrious men, although he would be allowed to eat what he wanted. He was to be examined daily 'for the purpose of determining whether long and protracted exercise causes a loss of vitality, and of testing powers of endurance'. All, of course, for the benefit of science: in 1872 Dr Flint would summarise his observations on the elimination of nitrogen from the body during exercise in a textbook of human physiology. All of this medical attention had the added benefit of boosting publicity and audience numbers and helping Weston's promoters raise that $5,000 purse.

The challenge started at half-past midnight on Monday 21 November. On the Sunday night, Weston weighed in at just 129lb. He ate a meal of steak, fried eggs, toast and stew with Ogden Doremus' son Charles Avery. Sticking to his policy of walking only on 'secular' days, Weston was played onto the track, accompanied by Flint and Doremus, shortly before midnight by the famous Norwegian violinist Ole Bull. The *New York Times* reported: '[Weston] was dressed in his usual costume of black velvet, white silk hat, blue sash, white kid gloves and gold-mounted riding whip. The six judges took their seats, with pencils and chrono-graphic watch; the word "go" was given, and he started off at a mild pace, accompanied by Flint and Doremus, but after passing the stand twice he quickened his pace and was shortly left alone in his glory.'

At 4 a.m. Weston went to bed, having walked 20 miles. He slept until 8 a.m., woke 'with fresh and lively spirits', and after getting another five miles under his belt, breakfasted on mutton chops, egg flip, stale bread and eight ounces of coffee. 'He walked with a free and easy stride of medium length with his head slightly bent forward.' At 1 p.m., by which time Weston had finished 41 miles, the doctors examined him and pronounced him strong, with no symptoms of exhaustion. He was unable to eat lunch however and carried on walking instead, stopping to eat a steak later. In the evening, the rink filled with spectators and Weston kept going until 10.58 p.m., completing 81 miles.

The walker was back on the track, in 'fine condition', by 5 a.m. on Tuesday. He ticked off his first 100 miles at 11.12 a.m., then kept on for almost five more hours, stopping at 4.05 p.m., by which time he had walked 120 miles. He slept until evening then ate more steak, with fried potatoes, coffee and bread. The medics again declared him to be 'in first rate condition'. That night he began his attempt at 112 miles in 24 hours, setting off at 10.25 p.m., aiming to complete the task at 10.25 p.m. on Wednesday 23rd. The *Times* said: 'He walked with a free and easy stride, frequently quickening his steps to keep time with the fast-metre measure of the music played by the band in attendance. Occasionally he would strike out into a very rapid and powerful pace, amid the applause of the spectators.'

Weston failed to make his 112 miles, complaining of lack of sleep and a sprained ankle; but even with the injury he managed 100 miles in 24½ hours, bringing his total so far to 220 miles. All that time, he ate only three boiled eggs and some beef tea. The doctors remained happy with his condition, noting 'the singular fact' that he had gained three and three-quarter pounds in weight since Tuesday, and that his pulse and breathing were regular and normal. A Russian aristocrat, Prince Alexis Dolgorouki, a Portuguese diplomat and the Rev. Dr Horatio

Potter, Bishop of New York, were in Weston's audience that night.

In the crowd the next day, to see Weston make his second 112-mile attempt, was the Swedish soprano Christina Nilsson, who had made her American debut at the Steinway Hall. Nilsson's later performance in Faust would be used by Edith Wharton to open her 1920 novel of 1870s New York society, The Age of Innocence. Nilsson 'greeted the pedestrian with fervent applause' as he set out at 10.13 a.m. at a 'lively gait' but, according to the *New York Times*, 'his step had lost a good deal of its former buoyancy'. The music of the band and the cheers of the crowd would, from time to time, inspire Weston to make a spurt and 'show his wonderful courage and endurance' but as the day wore on he became exhausted. 'Every now and then his eyelids would drop and the muscles of his face would become contracted, showing that nature was more powerful than his indomitable will.' He retired to sleep at 11 p.m. on Thursday 24 November. He had walked 43 miles in 13 hours, bringing his total over nearly four days to 274 miles; to complete his 400-mile feat, he needed to walk 126 miles before 12.30am on Saturday morning. The *Times* wrote: 'It is impossible for him to perform the task, however, although he announces his determination to continue walking today and tonight.'

The newspaper was, of course, right. Weston slept until eight o'clock, ate breakfast and started his last day's walk, to 'warm applause', at 10 a.m. His 'wonted sprightliness' was recovered following his long rest, but he had just 14½ hours left to finish his task. Still, he carried on walking, completing a mile in eight minutes, his quickest so far, and a large crowd stayed to watch. Many were still there at half-past midnight when Weston stopped for good at the end of his 320th mile.

Professor Doremus told the remaining spectators that they 'had witnessed the termination of one of the proudest illustrations of physical endurance on record, in sacred or profane history, since Adam was a little boy', and that he believed Weston to be capable of out-walking any man 'even in his present condition'. Doremus said that Weston 'had suffered considerable dizziness on account of the foul air and the tobacco smoke which filled the Rink'. He added that 'some of the biggest medical men had been utterly confounded at the great amount of energy which Weston had displayed during the closing part of his walk'. Weston had not taken a single drop of alcohol and 'his feat was calculated to offer a good example and to prove the benefits of walking as an exercise'.

Weston had failed to walk 400 miles in five days, he had twice failed to make 112 miles in 24 hours, and he lost the $5,000 purse, but somehow it all felt rather more like success than defeat. He had the resounding approval of a famous doctor who had called him a good example as he eschewed alcohol and demonstrated the health benefits of walking. Getting the doctors and the surveyors on board had been a wonderful coup. With their loaned credibility, Weston attracted a respectable, even cultured audience, not just the betting crowd, and the newspapers took him seriously as an athlete. Even once it was clear Weston would not meet the challenge he had set himself, he continued to attract spectators. The drama of the event, reported in the New York papers, brought local and visiting celebrities as well as middle-class ladies and gentlemen to watch this slight young man in a silk hat walk around and around a track.

THINGS WERE NOT SO SWEET AT HOME however. After all, you cannot feed and clothe a family with a doctor's pat on the back or a crowd's applause. Edward's marriage to Maria was not happy. All the traits that had made such a roller coaster of Edward's career so far, success followed by failure followed by success, made him a hard man to live with and impossible to rely on. In 1872, a newspaper alleged that Weston had requested a divorce from Maria because she 'sauced him'. It was probably a joke, but the conflict in their relationship was not.

TURKEY TODAY

AND FEATHERS

TOMORROW

EDWARD MISSED OUT on Wallace's $5,000 purse, but he had made $1,000 from his previous march at the Empire Rink in May 1870 and in 1869 he may have made as much as $15,000 (minus expenses) from his 50-mile showground walks around the northeastern states. In 1870 it was reported that Weston was still working as a journalist and editor; he might have managed it that year, taking on those few long walks rather than the many walks and weeks away of the previous year. In the US census of 1870, he turns up living in and owning a New York property worth $2,000. A newspaper from 1874 mentions Weston and his wife and children living near Macombs Dam Bridge, which still links Manhattan and the Bronx. The Westons' home was on the quiet side of the Harlem River in the Bronx, then a wooded area of farmland and commuter villages which had not yet been incorporated into New York City.

Weston was making generous sums of money: a lower-middle-class professional earned, on average, $2,000 a year in the post-Civil War period. But Weston's income was erratic; a win today could be followed by a loss tomorrow and another the day after, and anyway whatever money he did bring home quickly found a way out again. His elder daughter Lillian recalled that life in the Weston home was always 'turkey today and feathers tomorrow'. Weston was frequently in debt, and was a betting man too, someone with a tendency to throw his lot in with chance, the kind of man who would start a new career on the basis of a wager. Lillian's granddaughter Joyce Litz wrote in 'The Montana Frontier', her book about her grandmother and her family: 'Lillian seldom criticised her father, but she did admit he had one expensive flaw. He saw himself as something of an entrepreneur destined to make millions with his many get-rich-quick schemes that often failed. The fact was, if he wanted to walk he had to find other ways to support his family, and he was a natural gambler.' Pedestrian events were surrounded by betting and undoubtedly Edward was partaking, apparently without much success.

Elsewhere in the book, Litz wrote: 'Although Ed Weston just about owned the walking sport, he didn't make much money. Advertising was in its infancy and product endorsements not yet part of marketing strategies, and so prize money was his only income from walking. Some years he made a lot of money, and others were lean. He walked because he liked to walk, but this meant the Weston family often struggled to make ends meet.'

Weston did like to walk and so Lillian 'sympathised as she watched her mother pinch pennies and wait for the riches that never came while her father squandered dollars on his many failed moneymaking schemes'. According to Lillian, her father was dauntlessly, probably foolishly, optimistic, but to her this characteristic went hand in hand with generosity: 'From the overcoat on his back to the last nickel in his pocket, he would give, freely, generously, without hope of return. Naturally optimistic, he always expected things would come his way in time.' However, Lillian knew that one of her father's favourite optimistic sayings, 'I feel greatly encouraged', meant she should start worrying as 'he used it so often when the family exchequer was at the lowest ebb'.

Weston never changed. In middle age, he acknowledged his own financial muddles, joking with a journalist that he had written an unpublished memoir called 'The Autobiography of a Damn Fool'. He told the reporter that he had made $45,000 in one year in England but had had to borrow money to get home.

However, the problems in the Weston household were not just about money. Ed and Maria's marriage was not harmonious; they were temperamentally ill-suited. In 1928, a magazine called *Strength*, the in-house publication of a manufacturer of dumbbells, printed a feature titled 'Weston's Early Life', written by Lillian about family life with her father. By the time she wrote it, Lillian was caught in an unhappy marriage of her own, living on the edge of poverty on a Montana smallholding. The daughter paints a picture of two people living on completely separate clocks: 'Mother was very methodical, and ran her house like clockwork, and always had her meals at stated intervals. Pa abhorred rules and regularity, and wanted to eat only when he was hungry.' Time, she wrote, meant nothing to Weston, he was frequently late for dinner and generally skipped breakfast with the family altogether. He slept when he wanted, for 24 hours if he felt like it. 'In a way,' Lillian wrote, 'he lived "à la sauvage" in the midst of civilisation.'

An optimistic mind, like Edward's, might have imagined that Maria's method and his madness might complement each other: she seeing to the smooth running of the household while he turned his great energy to winning a living for their growing family. But Ed was far too erratic, their lifestyle too unstable and the distance between the couple too great. As Joyce Litz wrote of Maria: 'She was a conservative, genteel New Englander, a creature of habit, who clung to her routine ways all her life while Ed never recognised her struggle for an ordered life.'

Of course, the fault did not all lie with Maria: 'Weston never acknowledged the fact that Maria took care of the humdrum duties, duties someone had to perform, of running the Weston's family life.' Edward was not interested in domestic detail.

For her father, wrote Lillian: 'Change and excitement seemed as the very breath at his nostrils.' He was 'artistic and sensitive' with a 'Bohemian outlook on life' which he never lost. Lillian suggested that her father's feelings ruled his behaviour, but his freedom of spirit was a luxury that his family was not invited to share; at home he was the conventional Victorian head of the household. What Ed wanted to do came first and the family fitted in around him. According to 'The Montana Frontier': 'Lillian ... admitted in some of her writings that Weston was a bit of a tyrant in his home but always hastened to say he was outgoing and fun loving, never mean or physically abusive. It was, however, his opinion that his likes, his comforts, and his ideas came first before those of his wife and children ... He didn't adjust his life to suit anyone else, an attitude bound to sour a relationship.'

Weston's egotism, his great belief in his own ideas, coloured every part of his life and career, with mixed effects. Sometimes his views, for example on alcohol and smoking, were sound although they were ahead of his time, but sometimes his behaviour was just odd. In her feature in *Strength* Lillian wrote that whatever Ed did, he did because he felt like it: 'His appetite gauged the amount he ate. If he were hungry he swallowed a good square meal; then if possible, threw himself down on the lounge and took a nap. "Just like an anaconda," mother used to say.' He ate large amounts of butter ('Pa never ate bread and butter, with Pa it was always butter and bread') and preferred his meat and vegetables dusted black with pepper. He drank little water but lots of cold or hot tea as well as lemonade and other sweet drinks, Guinness and ale. On a hot day he liked to drink iced claret, 'but a glass or two of it would be his limit, he never made a tank of himself'. Edward would one day walk for the Temperance Society, but for himself chose moderation rather than temperance in that sense. He liked a little of everything, nothing in excess; he was no strict abstainer.

Weston was his own advisor on all matters. Lillian wrote: 'He rarely did anything unless he liked to do it, and would never dream of learning a game or any kind of accomplishment because it was fashionable. He was always keen to get all he could out of life, but he had his own ideas on all subjects and other people's opinions had little weight with him.' Weston pursued his own interests and had not taken up football or baseball, sports that had flourished in popularity during the 19th century: 'He could swim, and row or sail a boat, but there his athletic tastes and accomplishments ceased. He didn't care for baseball, football or prize-fights. He couldn't dance, skate, play golf or ride horseback, and I never heard of his going hunting.' He liked to walk but would take a lift if it were offered.

Lillian said that though he was a dandy, even on the race track or a muddy road, he was not interested in following trends: 'My father liked to look well, but he put a higher valuation on health and comfort than he did on appearance, consequently, though silken pajamas might be the fashion, his winter night garment was a red flannel nightgown, made long and voluminous, which he considered a preventive of rheumatism.' Lillian remembered an argument Weston had with a tailor who tried to tell him how the fashionable men were wearing their suits these days. Weston snapped: 'I'm not asking you what is the fashion, I am telling you how I want my clothes made. If you can make them as I want them, all right; if not, I'll go to another tailor.'

Likewise, he had no interest in health fads. He followed no special system or diet, 'never teetered on his toes while he brushed his teeth ... or kept the measuring cup and scales handy when he ate his meals', according to Lillian, or washed in front of an open window. He was meticulously clean, however: 'his clothes, his cellar, and, when he lived in the country, his barn and his chicken house were kept scrupulously clean'.

But while he was immune to fads, Weston did have superstitions, like lots of sportsmen. For example, he walked in the same pair of heavy, thick-soled leather shoes, much patched and repaired, for 28 years. In 1907, when he was reportedly broke, he refused an offer to sell them for $100.

Of course, one person's independence or 'Bohemian outlook' is another's obstinacy. During one of those times when Weston was failing repeatedly to meet the challenges he set himself, a Dr John B. Rich, a self-proclaimed 'expert in physical culture', identified Ed's stubborn self-will as the root of his difficulty. Dr Rich said that if Weston were not so wilful and would submit to proper training and dietary control he could achieve anything, remarking that Weston had a 'perfect physique' but needed to work on his posture and carriage.

But for all that Weston was obstinately determined to do things his own way, he could be easily and strongly influenced by external factors. He was emotionally highly suggestible. In 1876, the London magazine the *Sportsman* noted:

> *He is of highly nervous temperament; vivacious, but easily depressed; courteous, but (on these occasions at least) irritable. His nervous impressibility is well illustrated by the marked effect produced in him by a cheerful word of encouragement offered at times when he is fatigued. His face, evidently unconsciously, improves at once. So too, when the monotony of the walk becomes oppressive he will call upon the band to play one of certain favourite tunes, and under its inspiring influence he saves a minute on the time of the mile.*

Inevitably, Weston's personality was to be as great an influence on his career and his fame as were his stamina and speed around the track. Sometimes his tears and tantrums, his frilly clothes and attention-seeking might annoy his audience – and they frequently distracted from his athletic performance – but he was never boring. In the long run, Weston's tricky character, his obstinacy and temperament kept him in the public eye long after pedestrianism itself had gone into decline. Years after his rivals had been forgotten, stubborn old Weston would still be walking, still drawing the crowds and still amusing them too. But all that was in the future, decades away, and at the start of the 1870s Weston was still in a hurry to find the recognition he wanted.

CHAPTER

7

AN AMERICAN,

AN IRISHMAN AND

SOME ENGLISHMEN

DURING 1871 WESTON TRAVELLED A LITTLE, making appearances in St Louis, Missouri, and in Georgia where he made 50 miles in less than 10 hours. In New York, he made a second attempt at 400 miles in five days, again to include 112 miles in 24 hours and again at the Empire Rink. He had a new trainer, Charles H. Winans, and a new plan. He would tackle the 112 miles first, leaving him to walk 72 miles per day for the next four days to make his 400 miles. During that first 24 hours, he planned to rest for just 45 minutes, five minutes after his first 25 miles then five minutes every 10 miles.

He started at 11.30 a.m. on Monday 12 June. By evening the Rink was packed with spectators, and by midnight Weston had walked 62 miles. According to the Washington Patriot, 'every effort was made to enable him to complete his task. Ice water was dropped on his head, and his weary legs well lashed with a heavy riding whip.' Something worked, whether it was the new plan or the water and the whip. He finished 112 miles in 23 hours, 44 minutes and 45 seconds. He then slept for five hours, emerging in his velvet and blue silk in the evening to start on the remaining 288 miles. By the fourth day of his walk, 300 miles in, swollen feet were causing him considerable pain but Weston 'bore the suffering bravely, and his pace was unabated.' On 17 June, he finished his 400th mile in 11 minutes and 7 seconds, and with 15 minutes to spare.

After his success in New York, Weston fades from view for a few years. By the time he was back in the news, in 1874, America was into another of the depressions that came around every 20 years or so during the 19th century. On 18 September 1873 the financier Jay Cooke was bankrupted. His demise started a run on the banks, the Stock Exchange closed indefinitely and within a week most banks and insurance companies had shut. In New York, 5,000 businesses of all kinds closed as a result of Cooke's tumble: steelworks, clothes manufacturers, glass cutters, milliners and dressmakers all closed their doors, leaving their workers unable to pay rent or buy food. During the first, cold months of 1874, 90,000 homeless New Yorkers slept in the city's police stations. The trouble spread quickly to the rest of the US and within a year around three million people were unemployed.

In the spring of 1874, Weston was back in training with John Grindell, who had been part of his team during his 1867 walk to Chicago. Having ticked off 400 miles in five days in 1871, Weston was in search of his next landmark: 500 miles in six days, the longest stretch possible without walking on a Sunday. He would also attempt to make 115 miles on the first day and more than that on the last when he planned to walk 24 hours without rest.

The walk took place at the American Institute Hall on Third Avenue, New York. The doctors were there again, as judges this time, and were joined by some of the city's most prominent legal, business and military figures, including a Justice of the Supreme Court. Weston arrived on the earth track at five past midnight on Monday 11 May 1874, in black velvet and sky-blue silk. He was accompanied on his first few laps by his old boss at the *New York Herald*, James Gordon Bennett.

With Grindell on board, Edward tried out some new techniques to help him recover during pit stops. He walked 25 miles in the first four hours, took a break to snack on crackers soaked in coffee while Grindell rubbed his legs and another man bathed his head and arms, then, said the *New York Sun*, 'the pedestrian wonder was on his feet in six minutes and one second as happy as a bird'. Stopping another time, his feet were raised to a 45-degree angle and massaged from his feet towards his knees. According to the *New York Times*: 'Weston complains that blood becomes stagnated and a numb feeling creeps over his feet, ankles and legs.' He was still using whisky in his shoes to cool his feet.

The crowd grew as the day wore on and 2,000 people entered the hall during the evening. Each time the band played a livelier tune, Weston picked up his feet to put on a spurt, which drew loud applause from his audience. Each cheer boosted his determination and enthusiasm. Nonetheless, a pale-faced Weston stopped again shortly before 11 p.m. with five miles left to complete his 115 before midnight. After another rub down, he set off again, accompanied now by three policemen: there were rumours of heavy bets against Weston finishing and fears that punters might take matters into their own hands as he neared the post. He made a slow start on his last few miles, the first three each a little slower than the last, then took his watch in his hand and finished the last in 12 minutes and one second. The *New York Times* recorded: 'Intense excitement prevailed when Weston entered upon the homestretch of the last lap. He reached the winning post at 11 hours, 55 minutes, 58 seconds.' The *New York Sun* reported that $50,000 were lost that night in bets against Weston.

The next day he embarked on the remaining 385 miles. The *Times*, with a new enthusiasm for pedestrianism, wrote:

> *Whether or not Mr Weston is able to achieve complete success in the task in which he is engaged ... it is certain that he has already shown pluck and endurance in pedestrianism for which hardly a parallel can be found ... It cannot be said that this achievement has even been equaled by the best-trained athletes, and taking all the circumstances into consideration, the feat of Weston must be placed among the marvels of physical prowess.*

If Weston were a horse, the writer mused, he would fetch a fabulous price.

Where once the papers had urged the public to ignore Weston, now the *Times* complained that 'our citizens seem far too indifferent ... The example of Weston will induce our young men to use their legs rather than street cars, to the great benefit of their health, and the much-needed relief of the public conveyances.' It was true that New York's street-cars were overburdened. Designed to carry 15 people, they were frequently packed with more than four times that number. During that year, New York's 13 lines carried 150 million passengers, four times the number that had used the cars in 1860. Weston's friend Horace Greeley used to complain that the crowded cars were not fit transport for hogs let alone humans.

That day, Weston only managed 55 miles, instead of the hoped-for 85. By the evening of his third day of walking he had finished a total of 228 miles, having only completed a further 58. As the *New York Times* pointed out, he was now unlikely to achieve 500 miles as that would require him to walk 90 miles per day for the next three days and he had managed nothing like that in the previous two. All the same, on Thursday 14 May, the fourth day of the attempt, the *Times* reported that Weston had an audience of 3,000 ladies and gentlemen 'of the most respectable character, the mercantile and professional community being specially well represented'. The size of the crowd 'speaks well of the deep interest which the great trial of pluck and endurance has created in the public mind'. And, as ever, the women in the audience found much to hold their attention, at least according to the newspapers: 'The interest taken in the performance by the fair sex is something remarkable. They watch every movement of the great pedestrian with unflagging interest ...'

For the crowd's entertainment, and his own distraction from the tedium of endlessly circling the track, Weston threw in the occasional backwards lap and frequently changed direction. He clocked his 300th mile at midnight. To win the match Weston had to walk 200 miles in 48 hours. The *Times* thought he might just do it: 'That he will succeed in doing this seems to be the general impression, though the betting fraternity are of an opposite way of thinking and are wagering two to one that he will fail.'

On Friday, the penultimate day of the walk, Weston stopped to rest at midnight. He had a bad blister on one foot: soaking his shoes with whisky had caused an insole to soften and fold over, blistering his sole. He limped painfully from the track with 132 miles still to walk and only 24 hours to do it. The doctors found him to be physically fit but noted 'that his mind seemed to be perturbed by the anticipation of failure'. The game was up — there was no way Weston could reach the 500-mile mark now but the crowds were undeterred. On Saturday 16 May, in front of several thousand cheering spectators, 'and amid a scene of excitement not often witnessed', Weston's six-day walk ended. He had covered 430 miles, 70 short of his target. Even so, said the *Times*, 'he was greeted with the wildest applause and an eager throng of spectators rushed towards the judges stand to congratulate him. Weston himself was so overcome that he could do no more than bow an acknowledgment of the applause and by the advice of the doctors he was removed to his room. Despite the wonderful pluck and spirit he displayed to the last it was but too painfully evident that he was thoroughly tired out.'

He had missed 500 miles in six days, but his 115 miles in the first 24 hours was unequalled anywhere: Weston was the champion pedestrian of the world. The *Times* claimed that Weston had made more than $8,000 in ticket receipts, leaving him a profit after expenses of $5,000. He was also said to have made $7,000 in bets of his own: a good day for the family exchequer. Dr Doremus expected to 'deduce some important facts' from his observation of Weston over the course of the walk; Weston and science were winners.

THAT SUMMER, WESTON WAS ON TOUR AGAIN. In Philadelphia, he bagged 200 miles in 40 hours, spread over four days. At Goshen, Indiana, the local paper advertised the last appearance by the 'famous pedestrian'

before he left for Europe. Mr Weston would demonstrate 'his regular pace and his wonderful "spurts" of speed'.

Weston was not boarding ship yet though. He was still set on breaking 500 miles. His next attempt took place at Barnum's Roman Hippodrome in New York in September 1874, where he managed just 326 miles in the six days. Following that failure, apparently due to lack of sleep, some 50 Weston supporters, including those medical and legal worthies who had been acting as judges during his previous trials, wrote to Barnum begging to use the Hippodrome for another crack at 500. Barnum seemed keen on the idea; he telegrammed immediately then wrote a letter to formally confirm his agreement and to offer a purse of $5,000 for Maria Weston if her husband succeeded. The whole correspondence between Weston's supporters, Barnum and Weston himself was reproduced in the *New York Times*. It is possible that the letters were not genuine, that they had been cooked up by Weston and Barnum to generate publicity for the forthcoming event; both men were enthusiastic self-publicists and both stood to gain.

The trial started on Monday 4 October and Weston, wearing black velvet with a red silk sash, made a quick first few miles but never looked like he would succeed. In the first three days he walked 206 miles, an average of more than 68 miles a day but on Thursday managed just 16 miles all day. That evening, a reporter for the *New York Herald* was at the Hippodrome. He found Weston seated, his bare feet up, surrounded by doctors and other attendants.

> *They were all intent upon a black blister upon the second toe of his left foot. It had sat in judgement between Weston and*

> *Time, and decided in favor of the latter ... The physicians and*
> *attendants swabbed it with lotions and swathed it in cotton, the*
> *judges shook their heads at it dubiously ... In the seats above,*
> *scores of men and women sat with their necks craned eagerly*
> *forward, their whole attention absorbed in the contemplation of*
> *two swollen feet and ten inflamed toes.*

Weston's feet were 'the subjects of the gravest discussion and the wildest speculation'.

When Weston does get to his feet, finally and with a large helping of drama, he 'staggers, rolls and tumbles', an expression of 'intense pain' drawn in the lines about his mouth. Then suddenly, he throws his whip in the air and is off, with 'a strange, shambling, shuffling gait that suggests a drunken camel walking on hot plates'. The task ahead of him is impossible, 'two hundred and fifty miles in the two days left him are odds in favor of Time, his untiring antagonist that he knows full well cannot be overcome'. The band strikes up, his feet keep time and he flies around the track, slowing when the music stops.

But inevitably time was again the winner and Mrs Weston was not to have her $5,000 purse. The *Brooklyn Daily Eagle* wondered why Weston continued to command the attention of the press and the public while 'success would be about as unimportant as failure, in such a superfluous undertaking'.

What the *Daily Eagle* failed to recognise was that Weston's superfluous failure had been completely successful in one thing: it had redoubled the momentum behind his assault on 500 miles.

On 14 December, Ed launched his next battle against time and blisters. The *New York Times* had the measure of what was ahead: 'Weston was thoroughly cognisant of the immense pluck, endurance and spirit necessary to complete the project and though chafing under a sense of former defeat and public disappointment, he persisted in the assertion that he was equal to the occasion and the task.'

On the first day, Weston made 115 miles in 24 hours, finishing with just seconds to spare. Buoyed by this flying start, he briefly considered attempting the same tally the next day but the doctors talked him out of it. Instead, he walked 75 miles on the second day and 80 on the third. On the fourth day of the challenge, Weston walked another 80 miles, bringing his total by Thursday night to 350 miles.

Success was within reach. If Weston kept up the pace he had set in the last three days, he would easily make 500 miles by midnight on Saturday. Betting became fierce and Weston claimed he was offered thousands of dollars to throw the race. He became convinced that there was a conspiracy in the offing, that he might be attacked with pepper or chemicals by 'roughs' who wanted to stop him from finishing. The Mayor of Newark assured his safety and a warrant was issued for the arrest of a bare-knuckle boxer called Joe Coburn.

All this excitement brought flocks of spectators to the Newark Rink. It was in front of a crowd of 6,000 that Weston finally netted the 500-mile record, with 20 minutes to spare. During his last laps, while Weston drifted into a 'peculiar drowsiness', the whole crowd rose to cheer him on. The following week he was presented with a gold watch and a purse of $1,000; he probably made thousands more in some quiet wagers of his own.

There can be little doubt that Weston's failures at the

Hippodrome in September and October had been nothing more than skilful stage management. Weston and Barnum, the Prince of Humbug, had conspired to give interest enough time and encouragement to grow into 'wild speculation', drawing larger and larger crowds until Weston succeeded at last in front of his biggest paying audience yet. But that does nothing to alter the fact that Weston had done something no one else had ever done: 500 miles in six consecutive days, 500 14-minute miles. Edward Payson Weston had made this sport, these intense long-distance walks against the clock, all his own.

Meanwhile, however, new rivals were making themselves known and in the next few years Weston started to take part in more races, two or more men walking on separate tracks against each other. In Chicago, an Irish immigrant called Daniel O'Leary was finding his pedestrian feet, and soon his rivalry with Weston would capture the city's imagination, bringing Weston an even greater audience.

Daniel O'Leary had been born in County Cork, Ireland, in 1846, at the start of the great Irish famine which killed a million and saw a million more emigrate, many to the United States. O'Leary's family survived and stayed put until 19-year-old Daniel sailed to New York in 1865. At first he worked in a lumber yard in Chicago before travelling to Mississippi to spend a year picking cotton. On returning to Chicago, he got married and set himself up as a Bible salesman and claimed that it was in this line of work (strikingly similar to Weston selling his mother's books door-to-door) that he learned to use his legs. That and running to catch the swing bridge over the Chicago River before it turned to let the boats through.

Of the hundreds of thousands of immigrants who landed in America's ports in the mid to late 19th century, the Irish were the largest group (at one time a quarter of New Yorkers were Irish-born), followed by the Germans. Both groups were unpopular with those who thought of themselves as 'native' Americans and who feared that immigrants posed a threat to American values. The Irish in particular had a reputation for drunkenness, a stereotype which Daniel O'Leary would do nothing to dispel.

By the time Daniel started racing, O'Leary was already a famous name in Chicago. The Great Chicago Fire of 1871 was supposed to have been started by a cow that belonged to a woman called Catherine O'Leary (no relation to Dan). The cow kicked over a lamp and started a fire which raged through the city for three days. Whipped along by dry weather and strong winds, the flames killed hundreds and made tens of thousands homeless. Chicago was all but destroyed, but rebuilding began immediately and the city's resurrection would be crowned by the Chicago World's Fair in 1893.

O'Leary began his pedestrian career in 1874. According to an interview he gave to the *Chicago Tribune* a few years later, it all started with a conversation in a dry-goods store on the city's Wabash Avenue, the same street which a few years earlier had been clogged with handkerchief-waving crowds welcoming Weston at the end of his epic hike from Portland.

O'Leary's story sounds like the start of a joke: an American, an Irishman and a Frenchman were in a shop one day, chatting about

Weston's walk to Chicago. O'Leary says that his interlocutors reckoned only a Yankee could take on Weston and that it was mere 'Irish conceit' to think otherwise, though Irishmen 'could accomplish almost anything with their tongues'. O'Leary simultaneously proved and refuted the Yankee's last point, flouncing out of the shop with a verbose retort: 'Had Cicero and Demosthenes been born dumb, two great minds would have passed away from earth to eternity … without leaving a trace of their greatness behind.' Then he added: 'Laugh as you please, gentlemen, but bear in mind I will beat Weston in a fair contest.' It seems like O'Leary was indulging in a bit of 'Oirish' romancing, spinning a tale fit for the birth of a legend, or instead he could be making fun of the stereotype. Maybe it was a bit of both.

The saga continued: 'A Frenchman offered to bet $250 that I couldn't walk a certain distance in a given time. Nobody had any confidence in me, I had to back myself. I don't suppose I would have done it if I had to stop to think, but my blood was up over the jibing and I took him up.' If his story is true, O'Leary had talked himself into pedestrianism as readily as Weston had gambled his way into his career.

Dan's first walk took place at Chicago's West Side Rink in July 1874, when Weston was between his failed 500-mile attempts. O'Leary was 5 feet 8 inches tall, wiry and muscular. A sketch of the Irishman appeared in the National Police Gazette, a popular magazine that mixed sport and crime stories with pictures of dancers and actresses, quite like today's tabloid papers. In the drawing, his high forehead, thick sweep of black hair, dark moustache and lowered brows give him the look of a Victorian villain of the sort that tied young women to railway lines, although he lacks the black cape. Unlike Weston, O'Leary dressed simply. He wore a woollen shirt and dark trousers, and carried two short batons, one in each hand, for balance. In future races, he would sometimes use a couple of corn cobs as batons, as if to underline his 'salt of the earth' ordinariness next to Weston's frills. A newspaper report emphasised the 'very good muster of "sons of the soil" at the building', a contrast to the worthies and celebrities at Weston's New York events.

O'Leary's challenge was to attempt 100 miles in 24 hours. He admitted that he knew nothing about walking and took to the track in ordinary clothes and 'common high heel shoes'. The building's roof leaked and the wooden track became slippery but O'Leary persisted, finishing in a time of 23 hours,15 minutes. In August he walked 106 miles in 23 hours and 17 minutes, which, the *Chicago Tribune* declared, 'outdoes Weston or any other man who has set himself up in either hemisphere as the exponent of the art of combining powers of speed and endurance'. The Chicago press was delighted to see a local boy taking on a man from the East Coast, practically a New Yorker.

A month later, in St Louis, O'Leary walked 200 miles in 40 hours, in ten hours' walking a day on four consecutive days. The Tribune declared: 'Mr O'Leary's friends in Chicago are quite jubilant at his success, and in the sporting circles of this city he is and will henceforth be recognised as the champion pedestrian of the world.' In March 1875 O'Leary appeared at Barnum's Hippodrome, winning a 20-mile walking match against Wilson Reid, a New Yorker, for $500. Next was a 100-mile race against 53-year-old John de Witt at the American Institute, which O'Leary won, taking a purse of $1,000. In Philadelphia he walked 116 miles in 23 hours and 8 minutes, smashing Weston's record time of 115 miles in 23 hours and 59 minutes. The *Philadelphia Times* wrote: 'Weston will have to look to his laurels, for all of a sudden, in the height of his fame, a competitor springs up who bids fair to throw his best feats into the shade.'

O'Leary too felt that it was time for Weston to defend his reputation, and challenged him to a match. Weston insisted that while O'Leary had shown his mettle over short walks he would not meet with him until he had tested himself over six days. So O'Leary rented the West Side Rink in Chicago and on Sunday 16 May 1875 (he was not concerned about walking on the sabbath) started an attempt at 500 miles in six and a half days. A reporter for the *Chicago Tribune* wrote: 'He walks with a light, easy and graceful step. His gait is not long or swinging, but he has a short quick hip-step which gets him over the ground very fast. He carries his arms and elbows thrown far back, and head erect to give his lungs the greatest expansion.' Quite different from Weston's straight-legged step, bowed head and swinging arms.

Watched by a crowd of 5,000, O'Leary finished his 500th mile with more than two hours to spare. He was presented with $1,000 and a gold medal inscribed 'Champion Pedestrian of the World'. A few days later, the *Chicago Tribune* joked that O'Leary's triumph had converted the whole city to pedestrianism. According to the paper, the only passengers riding the street cars any more were 'a man with a wooden leg, some old lady of great obesity, a club-footed man, perhaps another knotted up with rheumatism, a very small boy with a big bundle, another with a load of pasteboard boxes, and a woman with a child at the breast and two or three at her heels'. Chicago was now the City of Pedestrians; the streets were full of men and women throwing back their heads and tucking up their elbows in imitation of O'Leary's winning style.

O'Leary's next two walks took place at the Exposition Building on South Michigan Avenue, nothing to do with the World's Fair (also called the Exposition of Columbia), but the home of the annual Interstate Industrial Exposition, which promoted business in the region. The building had opened in 1873, a signal that the city was 'open to business' after the Great Fire. There on Friday 2 July 1875, O'Leary tasted failure for the first time. His target was 150 miles in 32 hours. He set off, in 'light flannel drawers and short-sleeved undershirt' around 3 p.m. on a warm afternoon; the large crowd in the galleries around the track cooled themselves with ice cream and soda water bought from the booths dotted around the building. There was no barrier between the track and the audience, but police had been stationed round the rink and given the job of sending overenthusiastic fans and hecklers back to their seats or out the door.

Daniel started quickly, making his first mile in eight minutes and 55 seconds, his next two in just over nine minutes. By 11 o'clock that night he had made more than 40 miles and was ahead of his schedule. According to the *Chicago Tribune*, around his 50th mile, O'Leary's flannel drawers began to cause him problems as the seams cut into his skin. Still the walker kept walking, but on Saturday as he finished his 100th mile he was 'taken with a violent fit of vomiting'. The *Tribune* said O'Leary 'injudiciously drank some sour ale and egg and sherry during the night which disagreed with him'. He struggled on to make a further 32 miles by 10 p.m., when he was forced to admit defeat.

A few weeks later, O'Leary repeated the trial: same distance, same time, same venue. And the same outcome too. Once again, ale made him sick and he again called it quits at 10 p.m. on the second day, this time on 136 miles. By October, though, he was back on winning form, beating an amateur pedestrian, John Ennis, over 100 miles; O'Leary made a record time of 18 hours, 53 minutes and 43 seconds.

WESTON FINALLY AGREED TO RACE O'LEARY in November 1875. In the final hours of their duel, a crowd of 22,000 men, women and children crowded into the glass and iron Exposition Building, filling the galleries and trackside and perching on every clock, statue and rafter, to witness the end of a race which had started minutes after midnight on Monday 15 November in front of a few hundred night owls.

O'Leary had offered Weston $500 plus half the gate receipts for a six-day race. There was also a purse to be raised by the people of Chicago and the title 'Champion of the World' was to go to the man who walked furthest in the time given, or to the first to reach 500 miles. The race was started by Mayor Harvey Doolittle Colvin at three minutes past midnight. Weston, then aged 36, was in his customary velvet and silk and carrying his whip; 29-year-old O'Leary wore a striped tunic and white woollen tights and carried a short pine stick in each hand. Mayor Colvin appealed for fair play for the visitor and on the count of three the men began their walk on two separate tracks, Weston on the shorter inside track.

At the end of the first day the *Chicago Tribune* noted that the race was 'more likely to be interesting in results than in progress ... Walking is at best not an absorbingly entrancing sport, and for that reason there will probably not be a very large attendance until the last day or two of the trial.' The writer continued:

> *The style of the men on the track is very different, and from it one would judge that O'Leary was much the best man ... He conveys the impression of walking more nervously and with more exertion than Weston, and his crooked arm helps to give him an air of labor that his opponent's style does not indicate. The latter seems to drag rather than to throw his feet, and his long, swinging step, with his arms at his sides, is in strong contrast to his friend on the other track. The expressions in the faces of the two men are radically different too; O'Leary holds his head up and looks about him, while Weston seems to carry his head on his breast and to see nothing but the dirt before him.'*

A crowd of three or four hundred watched that afternoon; in the evening the audience grew much larger and included a 'delegation of ladies'. One man, who 'used insulting language' as Weston swung past him, was thrown out by the police, who were also kept busy turfing spectators off the tracks.

By 2 a.m. on Tuesday, O'Leary had walked 110 miles and was leading Weston by 20 miles. The younger man apparently intended to break the back of the journey in the first two days. He forged ahead and by that evening had made 190 miles and stretched his lead on Weston to 22 miles. Weston, far from being discomfited by his opponent's progress, seemed, according to the *Tribune*, 'intensely pleased at something'. Confident that he was still the better man over a long distance, he was sure of being able to make up the gap during Friday and Saturday, and made the most of the crowd's attention. The *Tribune*'s reporter wrote that 'his gestures, scraps of song, mimicry of actors, and other recreations, were greatly enjoyed by the audience, and seemingly by the actor'. Weston declared that he had never felt better and that by Saturday he would be flying like a bird.

The next day brought a larger crowd to the Exposition Building, keen to see the Chicagoan on winning form. O'Leary had increased his lead still further and ended the day on his 273rd mile, compared to Weston's 247. Edward's 'jolly good humor' persisted, as did his opponent's 'thoughtful' demeanour. On Friday, with just two days walking to go, the crowd numbered at least 8,000. The scores at the end of the day were 425 miles to O'Leary and 390 to Weston, who was still in good enough spirits to sign for a package handed over by a messenger who had chased him around the track.

By now, it was more than clear that Weston could not win the race, and on Saturday 20 November, Chicago turned out to see O'Leary claim his victory. The *New York Times* reported that 22,000 passed through the doors of the Exposition Building that night. According to the *Chicago Tribune*, they were a colourful lot; the crowd

> ... *presented rather the best and worst elements of society, with*
> *very little of the intermediate thrown in. As daylight waned,*
> *the crowd became slimmer, and between six and seven was*
> *rather light. But at the latter hour commenced a rush almost*
> *unparalleled. The approaches to the Exposition Building were*
> *surrounded by a surging mass of humanity eager to procure*

tickets. Excitement could not have reached a higher pitch, it would seem, for appearances indicated almost a wide delirium of the throng that besieged the building.

The crowd outside 'was dense; sweeping hither and thither, shouting, yelling and cheering ... it represented wealth, standing, and brains, and thieves, gamblers and roughs.' Meanwhile a mob consisting of the 'bummer [idler], political and gambling' element had gathered around the judges' stand, 'scattered through which a still greater proportion of thieves, rowdies, and pickpockets etc. ... plied their nefarious vocations'. The police were hard pushed to keep the crowd in order and off the track. Every possible perch and eyrie in the building was occupied. A gang of 'urchins' were seated on a fly-wheel at one end of the hall, and every so often the wheel would shift a little and a handful of children would be sent sprawling to the ground. A hundred feet above the track, men and boys were stationed, 'calmly, coolly and deliberately', on the iron roof supports. One group of boys who had found roosts high up on planks balanced between the roof supports got the fright of their lives when the planks started to sag and threatened to break or fall.

The crowd was noisy and mostly good-natured, 'pleased with O'Leary's feat but it did not forget to cheer the New York lad'. By 8 p.m., the Chicagoan was on his 488th mile, Weston on his 439th. Excitement and uproar swelled with Daniel O'Leary's every lap. The police struggled to keep the spectators from storming the track as their man came within ten miles of his target. At 11 o'clock he neared the judges' stand on his 500th mile and 'a terrific cheer rent the air, hats flew up, the band played, and the pedestrian's wife presented him with a magnificent basket of flowers'. He was also presented with the promised gold medal and the title 'Champion of the World'. Both men carried on walking for a few laps more, their eventual totals at midnight being 503 miles for O'Leary, 451 for Weston.

Weston had badly misread his opponent. The *Tribune* accused him of overconfidence.

> *Although he has a national reputation as a 'walkist', and set out upon the present race with the assumption that an easy victory lay before him, and was withal quite boastful and confident as to the result, he has been vanquished by a competitor who has hitherto had only a local reputation, and commenced the race with a quiet determination to do his best, and without any announcements or predictions as to the result. He has tramped, tramped, tramped steadily along, keeping to his work with steady persistence, while Weston has joked, and sung, and chaffed with the spectators, and taken delight in exhibiting himself.*

O'Leary and Weston each took home $5,500, their share of the $11,000 gate money. The next time they met would be in England, where pedestrianism had also grown in popularity. English walkers like William Perkins of London, Henry Vaughan from Chester and Peter Crossland from Sheffield had records of their own, mostly over shorter distances. The Englishmen should make easy opponents for Weston: a trip across the Atlantic would put his humiliation thousands of miles behind him, he could rack up some easy victories and win over a brand-new audience.

CHAPTER

8

THIS GRAND OLD

ENGLAND

EDWARD AND MARIA WESTON SAILED BY STEAMSHIP to England in January 1876, leaving their children in New England with Maria's mother and father, and doing in two weeks the reverse of the journey that had taken Edwards' forefathers more than two months in the 1620s.

Ed's name had preceded him and the English press was torn between frank admiration at everything the American had achieved so far and a suspicion that Weston's reputation, his 'recorded achievements', might yet prove to be unfounded hyperbole. The *Sporting Life* wondered whether 'Brother Jonathan might, after all, only be seeking to impose on the credulity of old John Bull'.

Weston was fixed to walk in a 24-hour race against the English short-distance champion William Perkins. Whichever man walked the furthest in the time would win a silver cup worth £60, the equivalent of around £3,000 today and buttons compared to the kind of prize money and gate receipts that Weston had walked for in the United States. This competition was not just about money; this was a chance for the Old World to take on the New, to put down the upstart Yankees (then well on the way to usurping England as the world's leading industrial nation), to prove that, after all, there was nothing behind the advertising.

Perkins was 23-years-old, Weston's junior by 13 years and, at 5 feet 6 inches, a few inches shorter. Neither man weighed more than nine stone, just a few pounds heavier than a racing jockey today, but Perkins was described as stocky relative to Weston, broad-shouldered and muscular with a short back and sturdy legs. He had been born in the central London parish of St Clement Danes on the Strand. The church, built in 1682 and still standing now, was one of more than 50 designed by Sir Christopher Wren to replace those destroyed by the Great Fire. The parish ran from Somerset House in the west to the edge of the City in the east and was bounded by Temple to the north and the River Thames to the south. It was a mixed neighbourhood; some slum areas had been cleared and replaced by houses for the wealthy but pockets of poverty and dereliction, corners of 'Old London', remained. Just west of the parish boundary was the dark and dingy Hungerford Stairs where 12-year-old Charles Dickens was sent to work in a blacking factory in 1824 in a tumbledown old house, alive with rats. The proximity of the Thames did not add to the salubriousness of the area. Once described by Dickens as 'an image of death in the midst of the great city's life', when William Perkins was born in 1852, it was the actual cause of thousands of deaths. Its bed was black with the sewage that poured into the river from London's modernised drainage system (replacing the practice of keeping cesspools beneath the floorboards of houses and emptying them by hand). Then the water companies drew water from the river and piped it to parish pumps, causing many of the cases of cholera that killed tens of thousands of Londoners during the middle 1800s. Whether Perkins was born into a street of artisans, into one of the wealthier areas of St Clement Danes, or one of the dark alleys where the very poor lived, the sinister stench of the river would have been an inescapable part of his childhood.

Sporting Life described Perkins, a specialist in events up to 20 miles, as 'the greatest walker England has yet produced'. He was reputed to be the only man ever to have walked eight miles in one hour and, in an exhibition at the Old Trent Bridge Grounds in Nottingham the week before his meeting with Weston, he had covered just over 18 miles in two hours and 34 minutes. However, the paper's confidence in the home hope's prospects in the race was shaky: 'Whether he succeeds on the present occasion or not, he will exhibit walking powers of the very highest order. In a long journey like the present the tortoise may, however, beat the hare, and the issue of the match entirely rests upon which man is endowed with the greater amount of physical endurance.' Privately, both men hoped to walk more than 100 miles in 24 hours, something which had never been recorded before in Britain. The *Sporting Life* said: 'If the feat is accomplished under the eye of the public and the sporting press generally, it will occupy a place hitherto unfilled in the annals of British sport.' Weston had committed to walk 116 miles.

THE RACE WAS TO TAKE PLACE at the Agricultural Hall in Islington, north London. 'The Aggie', opened in 1862, filled three acres and could hold 50,000 spectators in its enormous central hall and in balconies beneath its high, curving, glass roof. As well as athletics meetings, it held horse and dog shows, circuses, exhibitions and later the Royal Tournament. The building is still at work today as the Business Design Centre, an office complex and conference hall.

Between the dozens of pillars supporting the roof of the building is a clear central space more than 300 feet long and 120 feet wide. Here, separate tracks were laid for the walkers. Weston's shorter, inner track was covered with sand and gravel; Perkins would walk on the hard, bare floor of the hall. Weston's track measured seven laps to the mile, Perkins' six and a half. At least, that was the idea. When the walkers and judges — seven men who represented leading sports papers and magazines of the day — turned up to check the course, they found Perkins' track to be four feet short and Weston's three yards too long. The outer track was easily lengthened but fixing Weston's would have taken too much time. Weston 'agreed to concede the extra distance'.

The race began at 9.25 p.m. on Tuesday 8 February 1876. Despite bitter cold and falls of sleet, a crowd of 5,000 turned out that night, 'including several ladies', hoping to see Perkins beat the American. Weston wore a velvet jacket and trousers, white shirt and blue silk sash, high boots and a white hat. Perkins chose a simpler outfit: white shirt and dark, knee-length drawers. In his lighter clothes, Perkins took the lead almost immediately. The *Sporting Life* quickly took a position on the walkers' relative styles: 'Weston's style, as style is regarded in this country, is inferior to Perkins'. Weston walks with an easy swing and a short stride, swaying his head from side to side as he walks. He has a wiry appearance, is somewhat taller than his opponent, and walks in heavy boots and gaiters. His limbs appear to be exceedingly well knit.'

By 11.10 p.m. Perkins had covered 10 miles and led Weston by three-quarters of a mile. A pattern was set, the combatants moving in their separate orbits, turn after turn, the monotony broken only by a tune from the in-house band or when one of the walkers switched direction for a change of view.

At midnight, Perkins clocked his 15th mile and Weston his 14th. Paying spectators were due to leave the building at midnight, in line with an edict from the Commissioner of Police of the Metropolis, Lieutenant-Colonel Sir Edmund Henderson, who did not want the public to be able to access the hall's refreshment rooms during the night. However, the low temperature and an event elsewhere in London had conspired to allow only a handful of policemen to attend the Aggie that night. The harsh winter weather had prompted Sir Edmund to order that 'as much indulgence as possible' should be given to men on night duty; in practice, the colder it was, the fewer police were on duty. Furthermore, the State Opening of Parliament had taken place that day a few miles away in Westminster. A large number of men had been needed to police the ceremony, especially as the Inspector of Police had received an anonymous tip-off about a bomb in the House of Lords. It was decided that the threat was a hoax and Prime Minister Benjamin Disraeli, Queen Victoria and Princesses Louise and Beatrice were all present as planned.

The threat came to nothing but it contributed to a chaotic Keystone Cops-style episode at the Agricultural Hall. As the *Islington Gazette* reported:

> *It was announced that all visitors must leave the hall by*

half-past twelve; but though two or three servants attached to the building rang handbells violently for fully half an hour, few people took their departure. It was found impossible to secure the services of more than four or five policemen, owing to the number drafted off to keep order at the opening of Parliament, and, as may be imagined, these four or five had very hard work. Numbers of people concealed themselves in the gallery and other secluded spots, and a succession of chases and captures helped to pass away some tedious hours. Meanwhile the men ploughed steadily on ...

Eventually, the last stragglers were evicted, and only the judges and the press remained to watch; with a last flourish the musicians put down their instruments and left. The lights were lowered and the great hall fell into quiet and emptiness. *Sporting Life* noted: 'The only audible sounds [were] the tread of the pedestrians and the voices of the judges marking the laps and time. As the small hours drew on the pedestrians pursued their monotonous pilgrimage through the gloom like phantoms of the night.' The cold began to bite and the judges and journalists subsided into silence, bracing themselves for a long, uncomfortable night.

By 3.45 a.m. on Wednesday, Perkins had walked 35 miles and was the leader by 2½, but the pace was taking its toll. He stopped to eat a chop, take a warm bath and change his shoes, all of which took 30 minutes. Perkins had a blister on the sole of one foot and when he returned to his track, he was apparently slightly lame. According to *Sporting Life*, 'his arms were not swung to and fro with the same vigour that always characterises him when he is going strong', but 'he battled on manfully' and retained a lead of about a mile.

Weston kept walking, occasionally whistling for his trainer to bring him a drink of lemon tea or chicken broth, which he sipped as he walked, or ice cubes, which he sucked or else rubbed over his face and neck to keep him fresh during the dead of night. Then, suddenly, at 5 a.m. the dreamy quiet was ended, 'the reign of dullness broke and when the doors reopened there was a wild huzzah from those who were assembled outside'. The sun rose at six and an hour later the lights were put out. The audience grew by twos and threes as Perkins fought to maintain his lead.

At about 8 a.m. Perkins stopped again. He had completed 59 miles and 'his looks betokened that he was footsore and jaded'. By contrast, his opponent was as lively as when he started out, cracking jokes with the audience and pushing on towards his 65th mile. Perkins rested for more than an hour and when he returned to the track, he walked slowly, stopping again at 11.30. He limped back on to the track a few minutes later before retiring again, having walked 65 miles and four laps.

Perkins was put to bed and his trainer removed his shoes and socks, revealing the appalling extent of the walker's injuries. The *Sporting Life* reported: 'His boots were filled with blood, and when his socks were cut off, it was found that his feet were in a shocking state, being literally raw.'

Weston pressed on, weakening slightly but hardly slowing his pace as morning lapsed into afternoon. His 'movements were still as springy as before, his legs as nimble. His face alone betokened the amount of endurance he had undergone. His cheeks had now become hollow and his lips compressed and every hour seemed to find him growing older.'

Up until his 78th mile, Weston had not made a single stop of more than a few seconds. He had planned to continue without stopping until he had made 90 miles but stomach cramps forced him to stop for 90 seconds for a 'restorative'. He returned to the track but managed just one more lap before retiring again.

Here was a glimmer of hope for Perkins' team. Their man was on 65 miles with eight hours still on the clock. Weston was 13 miles ahead but might not restart. It seemed that a great comeback was on the cards for the Englishman, against the odds and in spite of injury, but the resident doctor brought the debate to a swift end: 'Perkins is thoroughly undone and unable to walk another step.'

Not so Weston. After 40 minutes' rest, he left his tent and returned to his sand and gravel track. Pale and unsteady at first, he soon picked up the pace again, throwing off his velvet coat and setting to work in earnest as he finished his 82nd mile. By now, the news that the Englishman was out of the race had found its way onto the street, but still the audience grew as people gathered to watch this extraordinary American racing now against the clock.

According to *Sporting Life*, 'the excitement was intense when, at twenty minutes past seven o'clock, he completed his 100th mile'. At this point, Ed stopped for eight minutes, complaining of a headache. To quote *Sporting Life*: 'He appeared visibly refreshed upon resuming his journey, having had some invigorating fluid applied to his nostrils and temples.'

In the last minutes of the match, the 'enthusiasm of the crowd bursting forth, the spectators rushed onto the verge of the track, and it was with difficulty that a clear course was maintained'. At 9.25 p.m., when the pistol was fired to mark time-up, Weston had walked 109 miles, 832 yards. It was not a world record, but it was the longest distance any man had walked in one day in Great Britain, and well worth one last lap of honour. Weston was mobbed by the crowd, then lifted and carried out of the hall and away to his Islington lodgings.

He was examined there by Dr Frederick Pavy of Guy's Hospital, Dr James Grey Glover of the *Lancet* and two other medics. They found him well, apart from a little nausea, with a pulse rate of 96 and temperature well within the normal range. His heartbeat was good, his leg muscles normal and his feet, with the exception of a couple of small blisters, 'were as sound as possible'.

The papers were beside themselves with admiration, vying for superlatives, trawling history and antiquity for feats that Weston had trumped. 'The walk of the American has no parallel in modern records,' the *Islington Gazette* gushed, 'and only one in ancient, the walk of Euchidas who went from Plataea to Delphi to bring the sacred flame.'

Weston's triumph put in the shade those of a trio of fabled British pedestrians of the past century. In the late decades of the 18th century, a man named Foster Powell had walked from London to York and back more than once, his best time being five days, 15 hours and 45 minutes. 'A marvellous performance,' said the *Gazette*, 'but for sustained exertion and speed it was nothing to the feat of the American.' Captain Robert Barclay Allerdice in 1809 and Richard Manks in the middle of the 19th century had each undertaken to walk 1,000 miles in 1,000 hours, but these feats were 'dwarfed by the marvellous endurance of Edward Payson Weston'.

As *Sporting Life* put it: 'Much as we pride ourselves on our national pluck and endurance and the invincibility of our athletic champions, in this great international walking contest we have to acknowledge a defeat, the palm of victory having been carried off by the American.' Britain had enjoyed several sporting firsts during the pre-vious two years. In the spring of 1875, Paul Boyton, the 'Fearless Frogman', had become the first man to 'swim' across the English Channel, which he did in a floating rubber suit, propelling himself with a paddle. Boyton would later found the Sea Lion Park on Coney Island, New York, the first permanent amusement park of its kind. In August of the same year, Captain Webb surpassed Boyton, swimming unaided to Calais in a time of 21 hours and 45 minutes. Webb would become a professional stunt swimmer, dying in 1883 while trying to swim through the rapids below Niagara Falls. In 1874, David Stanton had cycled 106 miles in under eight hours, then in 1875 he rode 650 miles in 12-hour stints over seven consecutive days. At the same time, reports of Weston's achievements at home in the United States had been reaching England but had not been received 'with full confidence, and therefore the hero himself came to our shores to give undeniable proof of his powers'. Now, Britain would have to be a little less complacent. The only consolation for the *Sporting Life* was that, after all, Weston was not all that foreign: 'so nearly are Americans and Englishmen allied in sympathies and blood as well as in speaking the same tongue, that it would be difficult to estimate an American as a foreigner, therefore we can more readily afford to congratulate our "American cousin" on his well-earned triumph'.

Weston took his success and the press reaction rather coolly. He had been sufficiently relaxed during his walk against Perkins to start planning his next challenge. In a letter to the editor of *Sporting Life*, timed and dated at 4 p.m. on Wednesday 9 February, a few hours after Perkins had thrown in the towel, when Weston would have been on his 85th mile or so, EPW set out his terms:

> *I hereby challenge any man in England to a pedestrian trial of speed and endurance, at the Agricultural Hall, Islington, to commence at nine pm, Tuesday February 15, and terminating at nine pm, Thursday, February 17. The party walking the greatest number of miles in the forty-eight consecutive hours to receive from the loser a silver cup, value not less than £50, and to be acknowledged the Champion Long Distance Pedestrian of England. Each contestant to walk alone, except when it is necessary for the attendant to pass refreshments. The judges to be selected from the sporting papers of London. And in view of the fact that I am in daily receipt of letters from both professionals and amateurs, proposing to walk various distances from 25 to 100 miles, I will publicly state that I shall hereafter consider no propositions for short distance trials.*

During his stay in England, Ed regularly based himself near Brighton at a hotel adjoining the Sussex County Cricket Ground and worked with a trainer, Jack Hopkins, taking regular walks along the coast and on the South Downs. This was where Weston headed to wait for a challenger for the title of English Champion to step forward. The man who accepted was Alexander Clark, a 25-year-old from Hackney, east London, with an excellent pedigree and, according to *Sporting Life*, 'the only man in England that could have any chance with the American' now that Perkins was out of the running. The previous October he had clocked the fastest time over 50 miles ever recorded in England, doing the distance in nine hours, 24 minutes and 16 seconds.

Weston's second race in England was to take place again at the Agricultural Hall in Islington, not many miles from Hackney, which in the 1870s was rapidly transforming from a satellite village of London to a district of the city. Weston again chose to walk on the inside track; Clark, remembering what had happened to Perkins, chose a soft, gravel path like Weston's. In front of 400 spectators, the race began at 9.45 p.m. on Tuesday 15 February. Clark, 'with a long natural stride, showing little effort', took the lead on the first mile and by midnight was nearly a mile ahead of Weston.

By next morning, however, the *Islington Gazette* wrote, 'Clark was walked off his legs'. The Londoner stopped to change his shoes at 10 a.m., having walked 54 miles, and never resumed walking, even though his feet were reportedly only slightly blistered. Weston, by contrast, 'preserved the unchangeable freshness which is characteristic of the man'. Through-out the whole day he rested for no more than a few minutes at a time, stopping to rest on an iron bedstead with his feet and head raised while his legs and feet were rubbed with whisky. During these stops, 'Weston displayed his invariable good spirits in a running fire of witticisms', chatting with visitors, one of whom was Perkins. Weston congratulated the Englishman on his performance the week before and admitted that if the race had been for eighteen or twenty miles he would have been forced to 'hire a horse and buggy' in order to keep up with him.

By 3 p.m. on Wednesday, 17½ hours into the walk, Weston had walked 77 miles, by 7 p.m. he'd done 90 and at 9.16 p.m. he made his century. He took a bow then retired briefly to scalpel a blister from the ball of his right foot. At 11.30 p.m., on 107 miles, he took a four-hour nap, the hall was emptied of spectators and the event claimed a second, unfortunate casualty.

While the hall was being cleared, a 'costermonger' (fruit seller) named Compton, who was thought to be drunk, tried to hide himself in the girders under the roof and fell to the ground, breaking his arm in three places and losing some teeth. The *Islington Gazette* reported that Compton was picked up 'alive, with his face frightfully mutilated, and insensible' and was taken to St Bartholomew's Hospital .

Weston was back on the track before four in the morning, 'whistling like a schoolboy'. At breakfast time, he 'caused a slight diversion by taking a cornet and playing "God Save the Queen"'. By 3.40 p.m. he had walked 154 miles and, in front of a 'wildly excited' crowd numbering 5,000, he hit his 180-mile target at 9.37 p.m., with eight minutes to spare.

He climbed the judges' podium to make a short speech. 'Though I have been walking in different pedestrian matches for eight years,' he said, 'it is only now on British soil that I have met with really fair play.' He gave one last cornet rendition of 'God Save the Queen', then marched to his lodgings with a large crowd around him, and led by the musicians from the hall.

ANOTHER WEEK, ANOTHER WALK. On Tuesday 22 February, Weston was ready for his third walk in Britain. Among the spectators were two wealthy and well-connected sports fans, one of them a future Liberal prime minister. Archibald Primrose, the fifth Earl of Rosebery, holder of a hereditary seat in the House of Lords, was a racehorse owner and football supporter. He was said to have three ambitions in his life, the first of which he would fulfil two years later when he wed an heiress, Hannah de Rothschild. The other two he ticked off in 1894 when he became prime minister and won the Derby for the first time (his horses would take the title two more times in 1895 and 1905). Lord Archibald was joined at Weston's event by Sir John Astley MP, a man who would come to play an important role in pedestrianism in the next few years.

This time, the race was to cover 275 miles in 75 consecutive hours, another step up in time and distance; a 'task almost super-human', said *Sporting Life*. Weston had offered a 50-mile start to any man who would attempt the challenge, but it was only days since he had been seen turning Perkins and Clark from champions into hobbling wrecks and nobody would accept Weston's terms. Instead, a man called Charles Rowell, a Cambridge athlete best known as a rower, said he would race Weston if he were allowed to 'make the best of his way', in other words if he could run. Weston agreed and the match began, another Tuesday night at the Aggie, at 8.05 p.m.

The 22-year-old Rowell set off at a dash, finishing his first mile in a little over seven minutes, compared to Weston's 12 minutes. The rower's strategy was to go out hard and fast and hope that Weston would be goaded to exhaust himself trying to keep up. Weston did walk a little faster than usual, clocking six 11-minute miles in succession, but no more than that.

After two hours, Rowell was four miles ahead; after three hours,

WESTON'S MARCH TO CHICAGO.

left A poster depicting Weston's 1,200-mile walk from Portland to Chicago in 1867.

right The front cover of the American newspaper, **The Daily Graphic**, New York, 16 May, 1874, depicting Weston's attempt to walk 500 miles in six days at the NYC Empire Skating Rink.

previous page A young Ed Weston, c.1867 and aged around 28, poses for a studio portrait in the year he walked 1,200 miles in 26 days from Portland to Chicago to became a household name in America. His first major walk had been from Boston to the White House in Washington for Abraham Lincoln's presidential inauguration in 1861.

right A poster advertises a six-day walk 'Weston against the world', at the Agricultural Hall, London, in December 1876.

left Weston is an immediate smash hit on his first visit to London in 1876, as shown on this cover of **The Illustrated Sporting & Dramatic News**, which depicts him requiring police protection from fans attending an event at Islington's Agricultural Hall.

AGRICULTURAL HALL,
ISLINGTON.

EASTER MONDAY
AND FIVE FOLLOWING DAYS.

April 2nd 1877

DANIEL O'LEARY.

EDWARD PAYSON WESTON.

O'LEARY v. WESTON
FOR

£1000

These celebrated Long Distance Walkers will Meet for the First Time in England, and Contest in a Fair and Legitimate Manner for

The Largest Amount of Money ever Walked for in the World !!

The whole of which has been Deposited in the hands of "Sporting Life."
Each Man will Walk upon a Separate Track.—Five Judges from the principal London Newspapers have been Appointed.

TWO MILITARY BANDS.
ADMISSION-One Shilling,

Matthews Brothers, Printers, Thomas Street, Paradise Street, Liverpool.

above The greatest rival in Weston's career was the Irish-American maverick, Daniel O'Leary. This poster advertises their first head-to-head in London, in 1877.

right **The Graphic**
newspaper of
14 April 1877 dedicates
its front page to the
Weston-O'Leary match.

left **The Daily Graphic**
of New York dedicates
its front cover of
21 June 1879 to Weston's
victory in the fourth
international Astley Belt,
held in London, and
the crowning achievement
of Weston's major race
career at the height of the
pedestrian heyday.

right A cartoon from **The Daily Graphic** depicts 'The arrival of Weston, The Pedestrian, on board the steamer Nevada' as he brought the Astley Belt back to New York in August 1879.

ARRIVAL OF WESTON, THE PEDESTRIAN, ON BOARD THE STEAMER NEVADA
RETURN OF THE ASTLEY BELT

left Weston at ease, a man of culture and refinement, away from the track in 1879.

right Weston is again in England completing a 5,000-mile temperance walk in 100 days, as shown in **The Graphic** in London, March 1884.

WESTON'S TEMPERANCE WALK OF 5,000 MILES IN 100 DAYS—HIS ARRIVAL AT
THE VICTORIA COFFEE HALL, WATERLOO ROAD

right Weston stops for a photograph on his trans-America walk from LA to New York, 1910.

below **The Boston Daily Globe**, May 1910, illustrates in cartoon form the anticipated excitement in New York when Weston finishes his coast to coast walk that month.

WHAT NEW YORK WILL SEE TODAY.

above Weston, accompanied by officials from the
College of the City of New York, sets off from the plaza in front
of the college on 2 June, 1913 on a walk to Minnesota.

below Edward Payson Weston, the world's greatest
walker, doffs his hat to his public.

the gap was six miles. This was a marathon, however, not a sprint and, predictably, Rowell could not keep up this pace. After making 20 miles in two hours 40 minutes, he stopped, resumed the race at a walking pace and carried on stopping, frequently. Weston did not rest at all, not for a second, during the first 18½ hours. During that time he covered 90 miles, took the lead from Rowell and then never let it go.

By Thursday lunchtime, heading for two days into the race, the Englishman was trailing by 40 miles and was effectively out of the competition but, showing 'an extraordinary amount of pluck and will', he kept going. And although the match was over, the crowds kept pouring in, 5,000 attending that Thursday night. Once again, it was Weston against the clock, and by Friday evening, with just a few hours walking time left, the clock looked like winning and there was a flurry of betting against the American. There were 8,000 people inside the hall, cheering Weston 'loudly and unceasingly' and running alongside him outside the ropes.

Before 10 p.m., Weston had completed his 270th mile, and by 11.02 p.m., three minutes before the 75 hours were up, he had walked 275 miles. Rowell had 'walked himself to a standstill' and covered 175 miles. *Sporting Life* wrote that 'there would appear to be no end to Weston's tenacity and nervous power' and that 'we have good reason to believe that at the present time there is not a man or horse in the country capable of covering so much ground in a given time'; his feat was 'one of the most astonishing ever recorded in the annals of athleticism in this country'.

Sporting Life was not the only publication to take an interest in Weston's remarkable reserves of endurance. The *British Medical Journal* marvelled that he had taken only 12 hours and 10 minutes rest during the whole 75 hours and had walked the final 80 miles in an unbroken stretch of 19 hours and 49 minutes. Even more remarkably, revealed Dr J. Ashburton Thompson, Weston had been ill. 'During the morning of the 22nd, Weston began to suffer from an attack of bronchial catarrh,' he wrote in the *BMJ* afterwards. 'There were a slight but frequent cough, hoarseness, and a little feverishness; his pulse beat with a force below its normal, and its frequency was somewhat increased ... but he declined to defer his undertaking.'

WESTON SPENT TEN DAYS IN BRIGHTON recovering from the 275-mile trek and from his cough, and preparing for his fourth race, this one an attempt to cover 500 miles in six days. With serious challengers thin on the ground, Weston offered £100, equivalent to around £7,000 now, to any man who could better him over six days or £50 each to any two men who could beat him by walking in turn.

Weston was inundated with replies but all cried off at the last minute, all except for two men, Martin and Newman, who paired up to attempt the £50 prize. The 52-year-old Martin was an extraordinary man, scarred and decorated during Britain's campaigns in the East. In 1854, during the Crimean War, he had undergone trepanning after a fragment of shell lodged in the back of his skull; as a result either of the injury or the procedure Martin developed epilepsy. In 1855, his sternum and several ribs were broken; then just a few years later he was injured again during the Indian Rebellion. After he retired from military service, he took up pedestrianism and running, setting records over distances up to 108 miles. W. Newman, for his part, had won some 20-mile races.

It was thought that this pair of 'veterans' would be Weston's only rivals. Then, on the Sunday night, a 32-year-old typesetter and former soldier turned up at the Agricultural Hall and said that he wanted to walk by himself for the £100 prize. Alfred Taylor had served in India, where he claimed to have walked 50 miles a day for six days under the tropical sun.

The race was due to start at five minutes past midnight on Monday 6 March. As the hall's big clock struck 12, the gas lamps were lit and Weston, Taylor and Martin (who had agreed to take the first stretch) gathered on the start line, Weston on the inside track, the other two back to back on the outside. Weston was in his usual finery, Martin wore a volunteer's tunic adorned with medals and a cricket cap, Taylor a frock coat, breeches and boots.

The signal was given and the race began in near silence, in the dead of night. Taylor made a quick start and took an early lead of a few laps. Martin took off at a steady pace but even so he fainted during his seventh mile, falling full length onto the track. He was splashed with cold water and revived well enough to carry on again after just three minutes. According to the *British Medical Journal* of 11 March, Martin had not suffered an epileptic seizure for months, but he collapsed three times during the race.

Weston took back the lead after 12 hours by which time he had completed a little over 57 miles. From then on it was Weston's race, as his opponents, to quote *Sporting Life*, 'subsided like mist before the rising sun'. At the same time, six miles west of Islington at the Lillie Bridge

Grounds in West Brompton, the English long-distance champion George Hazael was trying and failing to beat the ten-mile record time of 51 minutes and 28 seconds set in 1863 by another famous American athlete, the Indian runner Deerfoot.

By 4 p.m. on Tuesday Weston had walked 143 miles to Taylor's 99 and Martin's 68. At dinnertime he stopped for a fourth meal of the day. Meanwhile, both his competitors were advised by doctors that they were exhausted. Martin said he felt 'as fresh as a daisy' and kept going for another two hours before handing over to Newman. Taylor lasted until Wednesday morning, when two doctors examined him and pronounced that he was 'quite unfit to resume'.

Weston sprained his knee on Wednesday 8th, but still ended the day on 244 miles, which became 295 by 5 p.m. on Thursday, 323 miles by the early hours of Friday and, after a slow day, 390 miles by Saturday. He was hindered by a 'troublesome' cough but carried on, eventually completing 450 miles, an honourable failure. A Saturday-night crowd of 20,000 watched the denouement, which *Sporting Life* found a little 'gushing' for English tastes, rather redolent of the footlights than of the 'manly simplicity' of an athletic hero. Weston was showered with bouquets, he bowed and blew kisses to the crowd and, cornet in hand, led the band for a few laps before serenading the judges with 'God Save the Queen'. When a gunshot at last announced time-up, 'the enthusiasm of the multitude was unbounded', and so was Weston's.

As the *Penny Illustrated* reported: 'This great performance, albeit it fell short of the task which he had set himself, deservedly won for Weston an enthusiastic greeting, which so carried him away when he had climbed the judges' tribune and gave expression to the following highfalutin, though doubtless sincere, sentiment: "My heart feels more than I can say; but my prayer this night will be, God bless every man, woman and child in this grand old England."'

CHAPTER

9

PRUNE TEA,

BEEF EXTRACT

AND COCAINE

WESTON WAS DELIGHTED BY HIS RECEPTION in 'grand old England'. For the first time in his pedestrian career, he was being judged purely on the strength of his performance on the track; he was free from the American newspapers' obsession with rooting out humbugs. The British press also had a more relaxed attitude towards betting as an accepted aspect of popular sports like horse racing and boxing, while in the States betting was regarded as shady and un-American. Anyway, it seems that Weston had let it be known that he did not go in for gambling, and so far no one had argued with him.

The news that Weston had conquered London quickly crossed the Atlantic, where journalists were gratified to see their English counterparts heaping praise on an American. *Forest and Stream*, a journal of 'outdoor life, travel, nature study and shooting' hoped that Weston's triumphs had cured John Bull of his idea that great things happened only within British shores. The writer relished the notion of Weston 'in his old Hippodrome style' waving to England's 'proudest nobility', and remarked that Weston had 'done credit to his country'.

The report did, though, deliver one sceptical dig in Weston's ribs. Forest and Stream said that the presence of numerous eminent doctors during Weston's walking matches at the Agricultural Hall was his 'old dodge', imported from New York. As he had done at the Hippodrome, Weston offered himself as the subject for medical research during his races in Islington. In New York, the ploy had worked like a dream, a magic credibility pill that won over the press and the respectable classes in one go. Weston's London doctors stressed that he was motivated to co-operate in their research by 'a deep interest in the work', and that year Weston became a fixture in the British medical press.

During Weston's first two walks in Britain, his 24-hour race against William Perkins and his 48-hour walk against Alexander Clark, Dr Ashburton Thompson, later to become an international authority on leprosy and plague, kept a record of Weston's temperature and of everything he ate and drank. A physiologist, Dr Frederick William Pavy, analysed Weston's urine, measuring how much urea he passed before, during and after races in search of better understanding of the processes by which the body eliminates nitrogen from food and from muscle depletion. During his 500-mile attempt in March, Dr F.A. Mohamed measured and traced Weston's pulse each night around midnight. The results of all these investigations were published in the *British Medical Journal*, which stated that: 'The surprising feats of endurance which the American pedestrian E.P. Weston is now accomplishing in London are capable of affording instruction as well as of exciting interest.' The *Journal* added that Weston 'never bets or backs himself, and has a strong desire to make his powers of endurance useful for the purpose of furthering knowledge of the laws of waste and nutrition, and the investigation of the vital phenomena connected with muscular effort. Information on this subject is still much needed, and, when gathered, will have important practical applications to medicine and to physiology.'

Dr Pavy was the first to report back to the *BMJ* with a brief description and analysis of Weston's urine: amber before the race, straw-coloured during. In the next issue on 4 March, Dr Thompson gave a full report on Weston's performance during his third walk in England when he completed 275 miles in under 75 hours. To Dr Thompson, Weston was extraordinary. He counts out Weston's hours of walking against his hours of rest. During the 75 hours, Weston spent just 12 hours and 10 minutes resting or sleeping. His longest pause lasted a little more than four hours, his shortest 18 minutes. On the last day, he rested for two hours at the end of his 195th mile, then walked 80 miles in under 20 hours without stopping once.

Thompson remarked: 'The above figures are worth some consideration; for they speak with all the eloquence of facts, to the wonderful endurance shown by this pedestrian.' More important, however, than his ability to endure was his power to recover. Weston had been suffering from a cough and slight fever the day the race was due to start and was in fact not expected to appear. He insisted, however, and started out well. Then, during the second day of the match, Dr Thompson ordered Weston to bed after 100 miles as the walker appeared exhausted. He was very pale, his voice weak and husky and he had a wheezing cough. Weston fell asleep while his feet were being soaked in salt water and the doctor did not expect him to continue the walk. Thompson recounted:

But in less than an hour and a half he was on the track and looking much better than he did at his twentieth mile ... Great as Weston's powers of endurance are, it is not they alone which enable him to perform these most remarkable feats. Without them, it is true, he could not walk 90 miles absolutely without halt; but without the most marvellous powers of recuperation, a man put to bed in the condition just described could not get up again in an hour and a half not only looking but proving himself to be, as fresh as ever.

The doctor had noted the same phenomenon during Weston's second English walk when, at the end of his 100th mile, he seemed to be in shock: pale and cold, with a weak voice and feeble, irregular pulse. After just 10 minutes' rest, however, he was up again 'with every symptom removed'. Thompson commented:

It is his possession of this power of rapid recovery which distinguishes Weston's constitution from that of other athletes; and it seems probable that this advantage is such as must maintain him beyond competition. He possesses immense powers of endurance in the first place, and these may not be unequalled. He might, therefore, meet with a successful competitor at 100 miles, or even at 200 miles; but his power of recovery is so extraordinary that it would only be necessary for him to prolong the period of exertion in order to defeat any person not similarly endowed in this respect. Such an one has not been known hitherto.

Weston's mind had been under Thompson's gaze as much as

his body; where athletes today are trained to control and use their emotions, Weston's trainers worked around his personality:

> *His peculiar nervous temperament has to be borne in mind in planning a walk for him. If he can succeed, in a walk of this length, in making 112 miles in the first 24 hours, he is able to walk the rest of the distance at his ordinary speed of something less than four and a half miles an hour, and yet have time to rest ... But, should he not manage this, he falls into a state of nervous perturbation, which interferes very much not only with his powers, but with his capacity for taking nourishment.*

During the first, intense 24 hours when Weston was 'breaking the neck' of the race, he would eat nothing solid because he found he could not digest solid food, and would get by on a diet of beef tea, blancmange, egg yolks, gruel, coffee and 'prune tea', a concoction made by infusing plums in hot water. Towards the end of the first day, Weston told Thompson, 'he was progressing at the expense of his brain-power entirely. He had ... to think of each step and steadfastly to oblige himself to keep moving.' Thompson conjectured that it was this preoccupation of Weston's mind that affected his digestion; in the following days, with the hardest work done, Weston would eat cold beef, mutton chops, Peek Frean milk biscuits, potatoes, oranges, lemons, grapes and bread and butter.

Then, in passing, Thompson mentioned something which caused a storm of publicity and controversy. Writing in the 11 March issue of the *BMJ*, when Weston was nearing the end of his attempt to walk 500 miles in six days, Thompson commented:

At intervals, as he persistently pursues his route, Weston may be seen to go through the action of chewing; and a brown stain upon his lips, which the observant spectator may notice at the same time, lead to the suspicion that he is refreshing himself with a quid of tobacco. Yet it is well known that both during a walk, and for some time previous to it, Weston renounces tobacco; and, on these occasions, he is masticating a substance which, although credited with some of the properties of tobacco, is most serviceable of its class for use under exertion. That substance is the dried leaf of Erthroxylon Coca.

Thompson revealed that Weston was chewing coca leaf, the source of cocaine.

Nineteenth-century scientists were aware of the stimulant properties of coca leaf. An Austrian, Dr Carl Scherzer, had reported in the 1850s an anecdote about a Peruvian Indian who walked 90 miles in a day without resting, eating almost nothing (an achievement notably similar to Weston's own, two decades later) and sustained by chewing coca.

In 1860, Albert Niemann, a PhD student at the University of Gottingen, succeeded in isolating the active component in coca leaf, which he named cocaine. A few years later, a Corsican chemist, Angelo Mariani, gave his name to a drink 'Vin Mariani', which he created by steeping coca leaves in red wine and which he launched in 1863. During the next 40 years, his concoction found admirers throughout Europe as well as in America and, more slowly, in England: Mariani collected and published testimonials signed by Thomas Edison, Ulysses Grant, Auguste Rodin and Jules Verne, praising the drink for keeping them late at their desks.

However, so little was then known about the effects of persistent cocaine use that Weston's consumption of the leaf was not in itself controversial. All the same, the very next week after he first mentioned Ed's chewing and brown-stained lips, Dr Thompson wrote to the *BMJ* to retract his statement, writing that 'Mr Weston seems to think that even a qualified statement upon this point would prove detrimental to his interests'. He revealed that Weston had asked him not to mention coca and had affirmed that he had used the leaves only during his first walk in England, the 24-hour match against Perkins, stating 'that he had not seen a coca-leaf since his first walk'. Thompson continued: 'There is nothing nefarious, so far as I know, about the use of coca under such as the present circumstances; nor, I presume, would any person attribute all Mr Weston's powers to the use of some drug suddenly introduced to his system from without.' Leaving aside for now the question of whether Weston's athletic ability was boosted by coca, the immediate issue was that Weston's concealment of this part of his diet (it does not appear once alongside the prune tea and beef extract) made a mockery of the scientists' careful studies, particularly Dr Pavy's measurements of the composition of Weston's urine. Coca was thought to have a direct effect on exactly that which Pavy was studying, meaning his data had been invalidated.

Dr Pavy, of course, begged to differ. In a letter to the same issue of the *BMJ*, he insisted that his results were not affected, that Weston had categorically not used coca other than during his first 24-hour walk. Clearly rather peeved, Dr Pavy wrote: 'The elaborate super-structure, therefore, comprising the "coca-leaf theory", which implied the vitiation of the results of investigations I have been conducting, and occupied a considerable space in your columns, and attained extensive notoriety in the public journals, completely falls to the ground, inasmuch as it is only since the first walk that my investigations have assumed a systematic shape.' Weston appears to have either blundered into or to have given rise to a professional spat between the two doctors, one which would soon embroil one of Queen Victoria's physicians, Sir Robert Christison, and bring coca leaf to the notice of an interested public.

In the next issue (25 March) the *BMJ*'s editor stuck in his oar:

We hear that more than one person is prepared to support Mr Ashburton Thompson's statement as to the use of coca by Weston in his walk. There is no doubt that he chewed coca-leaf during his first walk, for that he acknowledges. He denies it during his later walks; but it is worthy of notice that it was during these later walks, in fact, during the last, that Mr Thompson observed, and reported in the British Medical Journal, the 'chewing movement of the jaws' and the brown stain on the lips, which led to the inquiries which elicited the information that Weston was in the habit of using coca during his walking feats. He has not yet stated what he was chewing and it is remarkable, seeing the scientific ardour by which he is possessed, and that every grape he eats is counted and weighed, in order to give validity to the laborious investigations which Mr Thompson, Dr Mohamed, and Dr Pavy were conducting in respect to these feats that Weston should have requested Mr Thompson not to mention his use of coca outside, nor should have communicated the fact to Dr Pavy

> *voluntarily in the first instance. Coca-leaf is, in its essential*
> *properties, it seems, not unlike coffee and tea, and there is little*
> *doubt, from the observations of that lithe septuagenarian Sir*
> *Robert Christison ... that it is of great use in enabling pedestrians*
> *to endure fatigue ... Pushed to excess, coca is said to become a*
> *narcotic; and we shall, no doubt, hear a good deal more both*
> *of its use and abuse. Possibly we may be indebted to Mr Weston*
> *for the introduction of a new stimulant and a new narcotic: two*
> *forms of novelty in excitement which our modern civilisation is*
> *likely highly to esteem.*

The *BMJ* went on to note that in the publicity surrounding Weston's coca use, the leaf 'had sprung into a kind of popularity' with the debate going on in the *BMJ* reported in the 'public journals'. The regional press had been quick to pick up on the controversy and reported to its readers in Liverpool, Lancaster and elsewhere that coca had 'marvellous properties' and was 'wonderfully nourishing'.

Some of the newspapers also reported the findings of Sir Robert Christison, who was the president of the British Medical Association, Queen Victoria's physician in Scotland and an expert on poison, who had experimented with coca at home in Edinburgh. At the age of 79 he was a keen walker. In 1870, he had undertaken what he believed to be the first investigations of coca's properties, testing them on himself and on his students by tackling long hill-walks with and without coca. The appearance of his name in connection with Weston's was to cause him considerable annoyance. 'Persons of whom he never heard, and who could have no claim on his heavily engaged time have written to him from all sides for further information and advice; and some ladies especially seem to regard it as affording promise of "strength and beauty for ever". The well known courtesy and energy of Sir Robert Christison have been severely taxed ...' the *BMJ* reported. The *Journal* appealed to its readers to leave Sir Robert in peace but revealed that he had been prompted to carry out new experiments on coca and that his results would be published in a future issue. In the meantime, the 29 April issue published a paper which Sir Robert had recently delivered to the Royal Botanical Society of Edinburgh on the effects of what he liked to called 'cuca'.

Christison said that he knew of travellers' reports of Peruvian Indians who became addicted to coca and withdrew from life to spend their days in the forest, chewing the leaves and 'dreaming of castles in the air', eventually becoming haggard and ill. Their families' efforts to wean them off coca might succeed for a short while, but the addict would eventually return, more avidly than before, to the forest and the leaf. Sir Robert thought this was exaggeration and that coca was no more than a harmless stimulant like tea or coffee, and suggested that its use might become similarly commonplace: 'If cuca is to be added to the restoratives of Europe – which seems not unlikely – it ought to be used at first with caution, and under close observation of its relative effect in several varieties of condition, such as age, sex, and constitution ...'

In his trials on himself, his son and two of his students at Edinburgh University, Christison found that coca leaf allowed him to walk further and faster without rest or food; he lost his appetite during his exertions but regained it quickly once he stopped walking, and his heart rate and temperature rose much less than would normally result from intense effort. He also discovered a markedly better ability to recover; coca made him feel young again. In September 1875, at the age of 78, Sir Robert climbed Ben Vorlich, a 3,223-feet Scottish peak. At the top of the mountain, while his companions ate lunch, Christison instead chewed some coca and rested for three-quarters of an hour 'during which I looked forward to the descent with no little distrust. On rising to commence however, although I had not previously experienced any sensible change, I at once felt that all fatigue was gone, and I went down the long descent with an ease like that which I used to enjoy in my mountainous rambles in my youth.' Later, at home, he wrote, 'I made a very good dinner. During the subsequent evening, I was disposed to be busy, and not drowsy; and sound sleep during the night left me in the morning refreshed and ready for another day's exercise.'

Sir Robert's experience bears unmistakable similarities to Weston's own 'extraordinary' powers, as Dr Ashburton Thompson had recounted them in the *BMJ* a few weeks before: his amazing power of recovery, his loss of appetite and its revival, his low temperature and pulse rate even after hours of continuous effort. There are other things too that suggest Weston could have been a habitual coca chewer. The cocaine user experiences emotional highs and lows of the kind that Weston exhibited during his longer walks especially; and while under the influence of the drug the user has an unusual capacity for repetitive behaviour, and what could be more repetitive than walking round and round a track for six days?

The *Lancet* mused that Sir Robert's paper proved only that he had 'coca on the brain', but some readers of the *BMJ* were prompted to try the leaf for themselves, including two doctors in Londonderry who corroborated Christison's findings and pronounced that the new wonder-drug should be 'justly celebrated'. The views of Sir Robert and the Londonderry doctors prevailed for the next decade. Coca-Cola, which famously contained cocaine in its earliest formulations, was launched in 1881 and during the 1880s pharmaceutical companies put cocaine in all kinds of tonics and remedies for sale over the counter. Its use as a painkiller and local anaesthetic was heralded in the *BMJ* in 1884. Then, in the last few years of the 1880s, the terrible effect of persistent cocaine use finally became known, in part because a number of doctors and dentists, even their families, had become addicts after they took part in ad hoc experiments like Sir Robert's.

Weston could have been using coca for a while. One of his doctors in New York, William Hammond, was an advocate of cocaine use and could have introduced Weston to the leaf. But there had been no mention of him chewing as he walked in America and nor was it mentioned again after 1876.

While Weston was stirring up the doctors in London, his great rival Daniel O'Leary was creating a fuss on the other side of the Atlantic. The Irishman was readying himself to follow Weston to England to knock him off his pedestal.

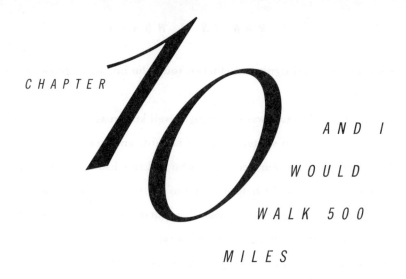

CHAPTER 10

AND I
WOULD
WALK 500
MILES

O'LEARY'S FRIENDS SAID that Dan wanted to be 'on his mettle' before he next challenged Weston. By way of preparation, he was walking the legs off every pedestrian in America, honing his performance over 500 miles. In April 1876, in San Francisco's Mechanics' Pavilion, he scored 500 miles in just 140 hours, four hours less than the six days he had taken to beat Weston over the same distance in Chicago. His opponent, Harry Roe, abandoned the race on the fourth day. But O'Leary failed in his next attempt a few weeks later at the same venue, falling 69 miles short. Henry Schmehl, his rival for this one, kept going for the full six days but made just 282 miles.

In August, O'Leary hit his stride again, though only just. At the American Institute in New York he made his 500 miles in front of 7,000 spectators. In the first day of the race, he was exhausted by hot and humid conditions in the hall and was forced to make frequent stops to cool down. Over the following days he coped better but did not manage to make up all the time he had lost at the start of the match. Carrying a heavy ivory baton in each hand, and subsisting on a diet of eggs, gruel, champagne and chicken soup, he hit his target with just seconds to spare.

Daniel O'Leary was becoming as well known as Weston and, like the Yankee, he soon started to attract hostility and attacks in the press. John Ennis, an amateur pedestrian who O'Leary had beaten in a 100-mile race a few months before, wrote to the *Chicago Tribune* accusing the Irishman of making pedestrianism disreputable by 'following Weston's method of hippodroming' – fixing his races, in other words. Another correspondent, Frank Clark, wrote to the *New York Sportsman* claiming that the track at the American Institute was too short and that O'Leary had only walked 272 miles in the six days. Clark's accusations were brushed aside and O'Leary was presented with a hefty gold and silver medal, made to order by Tiffany's, enamelled with the Irish and American flags and inscribed to 'Daniel O'Leary, Champion of America'.

In Great Britain, meanwhile, pedestrianism was flourishing, boosted by the excitement surrounding Weston's amazing performances in London, which had been watched by tens of thousands. The sport was becoming the biggest in the country, attracting the greatest crowds as well as the best prize money. As Weston travelled around taking part in races and exhibitions, British walkers were making their names and breaking records too. At the same time, Weston's fame and the excitement in London saw the sport taken up in Europe and Australasia.

In April, George Dootson of St Helens, Lancashire, beat Weston's record over 109 miles.

Then on 8 and 9 May, a 24-hour race was held at the Agricultural Hall in Islington. The organisers offered a prize of £100, stating that their aim was to test England's pedestrians and 'to see if England cannot produce a better pedestrian than the American representative, Weston'. Henry Vaughan, a 26-year-old from Chester, broke O'Leary's 100-mile record, making the distance in 18 hours and 51 minutes, then staggered, nearly collapsed and had to be led from the track. A few months later, Peter Crossland, a cutler from Sheffield, walked for 24 hours without a rest to make a world record distance of 120 miles and 1,560 yards.

A report in New Zealand's *Wellington Evening Post* showed that the fashion for pedestrianism had made its way south of the equator. A Mr Wiltshire had walked 1,000 miles in 1,000 hours, resting for no more than 90 minutes at a time, eating rump steak and mutton chops and supping on English ale. His next stop was Melbourne, Australia, for an attempt at 1,500 miles in the same time.

Back in England, at the Bingley Hall, Birmingham, Weston walked 150 miles in 38 hours and at the Trent Bridge Cricket Ground in Nottingham he marched for 12 hours without stopping, making a total of 55 miles. In April he travelled to Paris to meet some of France's *marcheurs* and at the end of May he took his first trip to Scotland, travelling to Edinburgh to attempt the same feat he had completed in Nottingham, 55 miles in 12 hours without a rest and this time to include a half-mile backwards. With great excitement and an outbreak of exclamation marks, an advert in the *Scotsman* newspaper announced: 'Today! Today!! Today!!! The greatest endurer living! Edward Payson Weston, the Most Wonderful Illustrator of Long Distance pedestrianism and almost Superhuman Endurance – from Scientific Living – the World has ever known, has been Engaged at GREAT EXPENSE by the Lessee of the Royal Gymnasium to give one of his unique and exciting illustrations.' For the 'low price' of sixpence, and sixpence extra for a reserved seat, the people of Edinburgh were assured of entertainment of a 'high-toned and refined' character. The Gymnasium on Royal Crescent park was a huge playground and sports stadium which had been built in 1865. It had giant swings, rowing boats and trapezes in the summer, and ice skating in the winter. In the athletics hall, 'velocipede instructors' taught people how to ride the new tricycles and bicycles. A track was laid out for pedestrianism a few years after the Gymnasium opened.

Weston set off at nine in the morning, in his usual velvet and frills. *The Scotsman* described him as 'a slight-built man of medium size, 37 years of age, with a careworn countenance'. Plenty of spectators came and went all through the day but the crowd did not really start to build until evening. By the time Weston finished the walk, 40 minutes ahead of time, 10,000 people were packed into the stadium, with 10,000 more looking in from outside.

After he left Edinburgh Weston walked in Middlesbrough and Canterbury, then 'the Great Pedestrian Sensation' returned to Scotland to take part in 'The Event of the Century'. Hundreds of fans were waiting to shake his hand when he arrived at Edinburgh's Waverley Station on 16 June. Weston's aim this time was to perform 500 miles in six days, including 115 miles in the first 24 hours, at the Royal Gymnasium once more. According to the *Scotsman*, he stayed up until three the night that he arrived, then until half-past two the next night. On Sunday evening he went to church with the US Consul, Colonel Robeson.

The attempt started at five past midnight on Monday 19 June, and went wrong almost straight away. Weston's attempt to walk 115 miles in the first 24 hours was knocked off course within a few hours by a couple of dogs that ran onto the track and tripped him up. Weston hurt his foot so badly he had to abandon the first part of the challenge, although he carried on towards the 500-mile target.

The weather was hot, but the pedestrian forged on, astounding the Edinburgh audience with his doggedness even when the sun became almost too hot to bear.

> At seven o'clock in the evening, for example, the look of the performer, as with soiled shirt and sweat-begrimed face he trudged along, evidently fagged, as was shown by the heavy way in which he breathed, was rather discouraging to outsiders: but when after the rest of fifteen minutes then taken he emerged from his tent wearing white linen and a smart blue scarf, with his face washed, and hair neatly combed, he seemed as if he had taken a fresh lease of strength.

Weston kept going this way, wrote the *Scotsman*, on nothing but beef tea, porridge and calf's foot jelly.

The weather changed on the fourth day, heavy rain replacing the sunshine. The track quickly deteriorated, and Weston's pace was slowed by the soft ground. The next day the track was submerged under 12 inches of rainwater and Weston was kept off it for nine hours. He took this setback in good humour, playing on a silver horn for the audience so they should at least have some fun, so he said, but he did not make up the lost time. Thousands crowded into the Gymnasium during the last hour of Weston's walk and at 10 p.m. the American gave up the race, overwhelmed in his last few laps by the spectators who rushed onto the track to pat his back and hoist him onto their shoulders.

IT WAS IN LIVERPOOL, the city where his younger brother Emmons had died 11 years earlier, that Weston finally crossed the 500-mile mark, at Toxteth Park on 30 September, making 500½ miles in 144 hours. O'Leary had arrived in England a few weeks before, and immediately began agitating for a match with Weston. Dan had been angered by suggestions Weston had made that he had 'not tried to win' during their great match in Chicago and that O'Leary's home crowd had not let him have a fair race, that he had been threatened and had pepper thrown in his face. Weston claimed he had been 'bulldozed', so O'Leary wanted to set the record straight. In his own words, it was time to settle a question: 'Who shall be champion pedestrian of the world?' His challenge was published in the sports magazine *Bell's Life* in October. He offered to walk against any man in England but with special terms for Weston, his real target. Weston did not reply yet, however.

By this time, 500 miles in six days had become the pedestrian gold standard, and both men set to work chipping away at the time and stretching out the distance, by a few minutes or miles. At Liverpool's Park Skating Rink, between 16 and 21 October, O'Leary walked 502 miles, finishing with 14 minutes to spare. The city's large Irish community gave him a hearty reception. So many people tried to get into the rink to watch his last few miles that the manager was forced to close the doors. In Manchester, in an event billed 'The Great 300 Miles Anglo–American Walking Match', O'Leary was pitted against Peter Crossland. The race started on 20 November at the city's Royal Pomona Gardens. Crossland collapsed before his 250th mile, leaving the American to take victory.

Throughout the months since he had landed at Liverpool, O'Leary had not stopped prodding Weston, issuing challenges through the newspapers and sports journals, and Weston had not stopped ignoring him. Then, at last, he took the bait; a provisional start date for a 500-mile match was slated for 18 December, but a proper agreement did not materialise and the date came and went. Instead, on that day, Weston began a six-day match at the Agricultural Hall, billed as 'Edward Payson Weston against the World'. Walking against three men, George Ide, George Parry and Peter Crossland, who would walk for two days each, Weston planned to make 505 miles but only managed 460. Ide, Parry and Crossland made a combined score of 488 miles and shared the £185 prize money. A few days later, on Boxing Day, Weston and O'Leary walked and lost in separate races: O'Leary against William Howes at the Victoria Skating Rink, London, Weston against time but with Peter Crossland and Henry Vaughan for company in an attempt at 400 miles in five days at the Aggie. Weston managed just 265 miles on this occasion. In February 1877, he was in Edinburgh once more, walking 55 miles a day for six days. A month later, and still in Edinburgh, Weston failed again to walk 500 miles in six days.

Weston could not avoid O'Leary forever, unless he wanted to look like he was afraid of losing again to the Irishman. Early in the New Year, arrangements began to be made and the six-day match was announced in the newspapers at the end of March. O'Leary was backed to the tune of £500, according to the *Chicago Tribune*, by Sam Hague from Liverpool, possibly the same Sam Hague who brought his British

Blackface Minstrel troupe to the city's theatres in the 1870s. Weston was backed by Sir John Astley, whom he had met during his first walks in London.

Finally, O'Leary versus Weston was on. Their first match in England and their first since Weston's defeat in Chicago started on Easter Monday, 2 April 1877 at the Agricultural Hall. Whichever man walked the furthest in the time would win two-thirds of the gate money, the other third going to the loser.

Judges were appointed from the staff of the *London Standard*, *Sporting Life* and two other sports magazines, *Land and Water* and the *New York Spirit of the Times*. They were joined by the Channel swimmer Captain Webb. The pedestrians each had a separate track and a tent where they could rest and change. It was agreed that there would be two bands playing and that the walkers would take turns to control the music hour by hour.

The start of the race was sounded at five past midnight. O'Leary arrived on the track late and gave Weston a minute's start. O'Leary took the lead in the first mile, however, and kept up his speed and maintained his lead despite taking frequent breaks. During a brief pause, after 44 miles and nearly eight hours into the race, O'Leary drank a mixture of seltzer and beer. He walked another 20 miles before nausea forced him to stop for nearly an hour. When he returned to walking, he made 13 miles before stopping again.

Weston did not take a single break until he had walked 73 miles. As O'Leary stopped and started, Weston walked steadily on and took the lead while his opponent was in his tent recovering from his beer. Weston kept the lead through the first 24 hours. O'Leary retired to sleep before

11.45 p.m. on 113 miles; Weston kept going until 12.05, having walked more than 116 miles in 24 hours.

Positions reversed in the early hours of Tuesday morning. Both men were back on track before 3 a.m., but now Weston was the one to take frequent breaks and lose his lead. By breakfast time, O'Leary was 17 miles ahead of Weston, on 148 miles.

As Tuesday turned into Wednesday the men had made 195 and 220 miles in 48 hours, O'Leary having the advantage. There was a flurry of late-night betting on O'Leary, now the 1–2 favourite, then 2–5 as he continued in good form. Weston retired at midnight again and slept for three hours. He had concluded that to win he needed to walk 520 miles and on this basis he had calculated how many hours rest he could take each day and was sticking to his plan, confident that O'Leary would overdo it and wear himself out before the end of the race.

By 10 p.m. on Wednesday, O'Leary had walked 287 miles; Weston had covered 274 miles by midnight. Over the three days O'Leary had not slept for more than an hour and a half at a time, no more than a few hours altogether. On Thursday afternoon, he was finally persuaded to take a long break. He had walked nearly 340 miles and was leading his rival by 25 miles, when his team convinced him to rest and he fell into a deep sleep. Weston kept walking but only managed to cut O'Leary's lead to 17 miles before retiring too.

The *Scotsman* newspaper noted the difference between the combatants' styles:

> *The two rivals presented a great contrast to each other in appearance, style of walking and general manner. O'Leary,*

who is a quiet, unassuming man, is tall and splendidly built and walked in steady, uniform style, and in continuous silence. Weston, on the contrary, is small and wiry, and varied the proceedings by exhibitions of somewhat eccentric pedestrianism, while he indulged in an exchange of jokes with the bystanders. His short 'springy' step is quite different from that of O'Leary.

The Times described Weston's style as 'the reverse of graceful', while O'Leary's 'comes up to an Englishman's idea of what walking should be'.

During the early hours of Friday morning, Weston's 'eccentric pedestrianism', which the *Chicago Tribune*'s London correspondent figured was caused by his attempts to wake up his weary legs, attracted the attention of the judges. Both men were required to walk 'fair heel and toe', never lifting both feet at once and placing the heel of one down before the toe of the other may be raised. Weston nearly forfeited a lap for his gambolling, but the judges decided that this one had been no worse than usual.

By now, Weston knew that the only way he could win was to keep walking. That day he put in an amazing amount of work, urged on by Sir John Astley. He walked from 4 a.m. until 11.45 p.m., when exhaustion forced him to head for his tent. He had made 83 miles that day, but had only reduced O'Leary's lead by three miles, bringing it down to 14 miles.

Weston was slow and stiff when he returned to the track at 1 a.m. It took him more than 20 minutes to walk his first mile. After two more miles, which took him 38 minutes, he went back to bed. Sir John Astley found Weston drained and emotional, flat with despair and exhaustion. Astley wrote in a memoir published in the 1890s: 'When I tried to get him out of bed he went soft, and on my telling him I should chuck some cold water over him, he burst out crying, and that settled the matter; for you can do nothing at any game with a party who pipes his eye.'

O'Leary walked through the night and by the morning was once more 25 miles ahead of Weston — only his total collapse could give Edward a win. The Irishman caused his friends a moment of concern as his walk suddenly became lopsided, but it turned out he was suffering from nothing more serious than a couple of blisters. After a short rest, he got back to work and clocked his 500th mile at 2.49 p.m. An audience of 10,000 had gathered during the afternoon. According to the *Chicago Tribune*, 'ladies waved their handkerchiefs and gentlemen threw their hats in the air, while the cheering was perfectly deafening for fully five minutes.' The ladies showered O'Leary with bouquets, making his tent look like a florist's shop.

The race was not over yet however, and both men resumed their circuits of the hall. After just a few miles, O'Leary began to reel and stagger and was led from the track by an attendant. Having passed the 500 mark, the worry now was that O'Leary could end up forfeiting the race in its final moments. A throng of gamblers and spectators gathered outside his tent, anxious to see if he would reappear. After half an hour, he was back on his feet and walked on until 9 p.m. when Astley, Weston's backer, called the match off with three hours left of the six days. Weston's total was 503 miles, O'Leary's 519.

In the last hours of the day, the crowd had swelled to 35,000. While O'Leary gave in to exhaustion, Weston was revived by the cheering and excitement and made up his mind to keep going until 510 miles. As the winner limped from the building, Weston had the audience to himself and was having the most fun he had had all week. Sir John Astley, wrote: 'I helped Dan off the track to his four wheel cab at the private exit, and he was that stiff he could not raise his foot to get into the cab; in fact, I lifted one foot and then the other the few inches required to land him in the conveyance. And when I got back into the Hall, there was my man running around the track, pushing the roller in front of him, and keeping time to the music of the band.' Weston finished his 510 miles in five days, 22 hours and 54 minutes. Both men had walked further in six days than had ever been done before. The *Sporting Life* reckoned that had the race continued until midnight, Weston would have won, 'for O'Leary became very giddy in his 520th mile, and it was very palpable that he was not capable of more exertion'.

Over the six days, some 70,000 people had paid to watch the match and more than £8,000 was taken in ticket sales, which sum the two pedestrians shared between them. A few weeks later, O'Leary sailed back to America with a cheque for $14,000 in the bank. It had, he said, been a 'good week's work'. In an interview with the *New York Sun* in the 1880s he described it as the high point of his career: 'Since then I have given a few exhibitions but have had no matches of importance.'

It had been a good week for someone else too. Sir John Astley wrote: 'Out of the 142 hours, O'Leary had only been off the track 26 hours, and Weston 28 hours. For that matter, I don't believe I had more than two or three hours sleep myself in each twenty-four, for I never was more excited over any performance; and the number of cigars I got through was a record — not silly little female cigarettes either.'

11

THIS

INDOMITABLE

STAYER

SIR JOHN ASTLEY, WITH HIS BIG, MANLY CIGARS, was so excited by pedestrianism that he decided to lend his name to a series of six-day races to find the Long Distance Champion of the World. At the age of 50, Sir John Dugdale Astley, 3rd Baronet, had been a liberal MP for four years but was best known for his passion for sport, especially racing and boxing, and for the large sums of money that he won and lost in bets. He had been an athlete himself as a young man, winning various cups for running in the 1850s, a few years after he had fought and been wounded in the Crimea.

In February 1876 Astley had turned up with his friend the Earl of Rosebery at Weston's race against Charles Rowell and had been impressed both by the American walker and the enthusiastic, and enthusiastically betting, audience. He became friends with Edward, backed him in several of his subsequent competitions and watched pedestrianism grow in popularity.

In the latter half of 1877, Weston was on tour, appearing in races and exhibitions in front of thousands in Newcastle, Glasgow, Bradford,

Bristol and Hull. In August, in a large tent in the Northumberland Cricket Ground in Newcastle, Weston clocked 400 miles in five days, crossing the finish line in front of a crowd of 3,500. He was not the only walker attracting a big audience. In May 1877, 2,000 people watched Peter Crossland and Harry Vaughan in a 48-hour match in which Crossland made 174 miles and Vaughan 191. Then, in London, 6,000 gathered to see William Gale of Cardiff tackle the last few miles of an attempt at 1,500 miles in 1,000 hours. By the final few days, Gale was suffering pain from varicose veins and a groin strain and was so tired he kept drifting into sleep and falling flat on his face while he walked. Sir John was there with some friends and was so struck by the man's courage that he helped fill a purse for the Welshman.

Pedestrianism was nearing the height of its popularity in the UK and America. Events were taking place all over the country and athletes made up their own rules and picked their own times and distances. While there were some who preferred short sharp races, like William Howes, who walked 21 miles in three hours in Edinburgh in April 1877, there were plenty more, like William Gale, who took the opposite tack and made the sport into a test not of speed but of how far they could journey into exhaustion and still keep moving. While the sporting press tabulated each mile and minute of these extraordinary events, other voices in the British press were expressing alarm. After Weston's match with O'Leary in London, one magazine described long pedestrian races as a slow suicide watched and condoned by respectable society:

> *A modern walking match attended by doctors, priests, ladies,*
> *and the representatives of English pluck, is about the most*

sickening spectacle that could be devised by a nation indignant at cockfighting, and virtuously outraged at vivisection. Words could not well describe the painful sight of American athletes half delirious from want of sleep, half hysterical with tortured nerves ... Let us have no more of these matches, lest, encouraged by the mercenary applause, the bow is bent too far and the thin string of life is cracked. The doctors, the priests, and the noble sportsmen would not care to see O'Leary drop down dead on the track, or to see Weston walking over the brink of his grave and into it.

In Sunderland in October 1877, a man called William Hunter did drop dead the day after he had tackled one of Weston's records. Hunter attempted one of Weston's performances, 150 miles in two days. He exceeded his target by ten miles but then died suddenly the next afternoon.

Astley was undeterred. At the beginning of 1878 he had a prize made for the winner of his race, a heavy, ornate belt crafted from silver, leather and gold plate, engraved with images of two men, one running, one walking, and the title 'Long Distance Champion of the World'. The inaugural race, which became known as the First International Astley Belt, was announced for March 1878 and the arrangements for the event published in *Sporting Life*. To enter, every competitor was obliged to lodge a £100 stake with Charles Conquest of *Sporting Life*. The winner would be the man who walked furthest in the six days. The victor would have to defend his title not more often than once every six months, and would become the permanent title-holder if he won three times in a row. If the belt was won by a foreigner, he could choose to take it home with him and the next challenge could be held in the winner's home country. In practice, foreign meant American, and over the next year or two, pedestrianism became a transatlantic business with British and American walkers crossing the ocean in both directions to challenge for the belt and then carry it home in victory.

Astley made one important change from previous races. Whereas before competitors had generally been required to show a 'fair heel and toe' style, one heel hitting the ground before the toes of the other foot are lifted, the Astley Belt was to be different. The theme was 'go as you please' and entrants were encouraged to 'walk, run, mix, trot or introduce a new style of pedestrianism if clever enough'. There were two reasons for this move: first, it meant that Weston, whose 'wobbly' walking style had been queried in heel and toe races, would be free from doubt; second, it was hoped that if the English athletes were allowed to run they might stand a better chance of beating the Americans who had utterly dominated every race so far. As it turned out, 'go as you please' had some unexpected consequences.

THE FIRST INTERNATIONAL ASTLEY BELT took place at the Agricultural Hall on Monday 18 March 1878. Each contestant had been provided with a 'hut' containing a bed and a stove. The *Sporting Life* claimed that the huts were unfit, that they had recently been used as stabling for camels when John and George Sanger's circus was leasing the hall, and that they still smelled of the beasts.

Two tracks were laid, one for British walkers and one for

foreigners. In this instance 15 Englishmen, one Irishman and two Scots shared the shorter inside track and one foreigner had the outside track to himself. Four Londoners, William 'Corkey' Gentleman, George Hazael, George Ide and Henry Brown, as well as Chester's Henry Vaughan lined up among the British men. The man with the 'foreign' rink to himself was Dan O'Leary, who had sailed from New York with his wife for a chance at the title. The name E.P. Weston was absent; he was ill and unable to compete, prompting the *New York Times* to ask: 'Is Weston afraid of O'Leary?'

At one in the morning, as the race was about to begin, Sir John Astley said a few words to the walkers: 'You are about to enter in a trying match, in which running and walking and physical pluck and endurance are necessary to compete. Every possible arrangement has been made to have a fair, straight fight, and I hope the best man will win. I appeal to you to second our efforts, for the best man to win, no matter what his nationality, or where he come from. Now lads, are you ready? A fair, honest, manly race and the best man wins. Ready? Then away you go!' At three minutes past one, away they went.

There was a huge amount of betting before the race, with Henry Vaughan the 5–3 favourite: if he won, the bookies would lose around £100,000, something like £7 million today. In the first minutes, the lead was taken by William Smith, followed by Corkey, then Brown, Vaughan and O'Leary. A little behind O'Leary was George Hazael, walking in the opposite direction to everyone else. Ten miles in, Hazael overtook O'Leary and started trying to intimidate him, shouting at him every time they passed on the track, even threatening to kill him. O'Leary began to run and soon took the lead from Hazael, who anyway dropped out of the match after 50 miles.

During the first two days, the race was dominated by four men: Corkey Gentleman, the smallest and at 45 the oldest walker, Vaughan, Brown and O'Leary. The *Penny Illustrated* sketched the leaders during the first day. Corkey Gentleman, who made a meagre living selling cat food door-to-door in the East End of London, comes across like a character in a Dickens novel, a miniature Bob Cratchit 'whom a breath could blow away' and who astounded everyone by standing up to Dan O'Leary:

> *... little Corkey bounded over the turf by himself ... reminding one of those wan little fathers of large families who humbly and meekly walk to and from the City every day of their weary lives, to bring up their too plentiful olive branches with credit. Looking at Corkey, then, as he untiringly ran around the hall, no one could have dreamt that for the first day or so, Corkey led the famous O'Leary a good dance, and even led the Hibernian American, who trod the earth so firmly that he appeared at times as desirous of stamping the turf flat as of progressing to the 500 miles goal. Now and then, the heavily built O'Leary burst into a run on the corners; but he walked fairly and squarely for the most part, throwing his head back and moving his arms freely. Handsomest of all was Vaughan, whose style of walking was a model of machine gun regularity.*

The *Sporting Life* described 'Blower' Brown, a brick maker, as 'plucky and persevering' and remarked that 'this wonderful little man has a pace exactly modelled somewhat [on] the reputed speed of a pig, an animal which is popularly supposed to go just a little faster than anything that tries to catch it.'

The Agricultural Hall was closed to spectators through the night, but thousands crowded the galleries each day to see how the race was going. By the end of the fourth day, only nine men were still on their feet, and the contest had become a battle between Vaughan and O'Leary. On Friday, the penultimate day, Vaughan was trailing O'Leary by 14 miles but looked to be the stronger walker. A crowd of 10,000 watched as Vaughan, on his 400th mile, decided to try to reduce O'Leary's lead and began 'doubling' laps, that is walking along the straights and trotting on the bends, perfectly acceptable in Astley's 'go as you please' match. Dan, meanwhile, walked with trembling knees and, according to *Sporting Life*, showed 'great signs of fatigue, though he never has for one moment flinched from his work'. When the Hall was cleared at 11.30 that night, O'Leary was on 457 miles, Vaughan was on 441, and the next walker, Brown, was 25 miles behind him.

The next day, the last of the race, O'Leary held his lead but looked weaker even than the day before. Sir John Astley wrote in his memoir that O'Leary became so dazed he could not see the edge of the track, until fresh white sawdust was brought and laid around the edge. The race was called to a halt nearly five hours early, after so many of the 15,000 spectators swarmed onto the tracks that the walkers could not keep going. O'Leary had won it, having made 520 miles and two laps, but he was 'haggard, dazed, staggering'.

O'Leary carried Astley's gold and silver belt home to Chicago where he told reporters that he would try to hold on to the title. He reckoned that the competition would get tougher and told the journalists that whoever won the next Astley Belt Race would have to walk 600 miles, adding 'there will be at least one corpse on the track'. As it happened, his prediction was a long way off the mark and the second International Belt turned out to be what the newspapers might have called a fizzle, but in the longer term he was on the right lines. Allowing running and trotting in pedestrian races notched up the distance the competitors covered with each race and the athletes had to work harder and harder to win.

THE SECOND INTERNATIONAL ASTLEY BELT RACE took place in New York from Monday 30 September to Saturday 5 October 1878. O'Leary had just one challenger, an illiterate Irish day-labourer called John Hughes who reckoned he could outrun any man in the world but until now had been 'too poor, ignorant and unknown' to find a backer. Born in County Tipperary in 1850, Hughes was said to be stronger and brawnier than O'Leary and more than his equal in Irishness. A reporter for the *Chicago Tribune* wrote that Hughes was 'about the Irishest man I ever saw, and if his traveling wind is as lasting as that which he consumes in talk, he ought to run a year at top speed'.

Somehow, Hughes had come into contact with Harry Hill, the owner of a famous saloon near Broadway in New York's Bowery district. At Harry Hill's, politicians, doctors and judges drank with boxers and showgirls while the police turned a blind eye. Thomas Edison was a regular and personally installed the saloon's first light bulbs when New York's night life went electric in the 1880s. Hill offered Hughes $500 if he could beat O'Leary's London record of 520 miles in six days. Hughes failed miserably and Hill dropped him but the Irishman found three more backers willing to help him race O'Leary.

The match took place at Gilmore's Concert Garden on the site that had been Barnum's Hippodrome and was to become, a few years later, the first Madison Square Garden. The two men had the customary tents in the arena and Hughes's wife and young son Willy camped in his tent throughout the six days. Willy would sit outside the tent and cheer his father on while his mother was inside cooking up chicken stew and beef tea.

Almost as soon as the race started O'Leary opened up a clear lead from Hughes and there was little doubt of who would be the winner, but the race still attracted crowds of 5,000 and more each day. On the final day, in front of a crowd of 7,000, O'Leary won the second Astley International Belt with a relatively low score of 403 miles to Hughes's 310. O'Leary admitted that the race had been a walkover, and that with a better opponent he would have walked further. Hughes later went to court to complain that his backers had taken advantage of his illiteracy and had tricked him into giving them power of attorney so they could collect his winnings.

IN BRITAIN, MEANWHILE, with the International Belt apparently stuck in America, Sir John Astley launched a new event, a six-day Long Distance Championship of England. First prize was £500 plus the newly minted Challenge Belt worth £100, and conditions were to be the same as they had been for the international competition in March except that any rematch must take place in England and this time there would be no separation of British and foreign competitors; all would walk on the same track. After O'Leary's victory, British journalists had complained that the American had had an unfair advantage as his track had stayed in good condition while the British track quickly deteriorated under so many pairs of boots.

The new event took place at the Agricultural Hall between Monday 28 October and Saturday 2nd November 1878. There were 23 competitors, including Weston and two more Americans, John Ennis and W.S. Richardson. Sheffield's Peter Crossland was there, along with three of the stars of the first International Astley Belt, Henry Vaughan, Corkey Gentleman and Henry Brown.

Weston and Vaughan started the race as favourites but it was Brown who took the lead in the first mile and held it for the first 12 hours, with Vaughan in third place, Crossland in fourth, Weston in sixth and Corkey eighth. By the early evening, 10,000 people had made their way to the hall to watch the 23 men walk, jog and run round the track. Brown was the first to clock 100 miles, doing it in a record time of 17 hours and 54 minutes, before going to bed a few miles later, leaving Crossland to take the lead by the time the public were sent home for the night.

Crossland and Corkey stayed up all night battling for lead position, first one striking out in front, then the other. The two continued to share the lead all through the second day of the race and the *Sportsman* complained that there was not much excitement to be had for the spectators. Exciting or not, it was a fast race. At 10.40 p.m. Corkey became the first man to break 200 miles, with Brown and Crossland just a few minutes behind him, all three beating by 13 hours the time that O'Leary had taken to walk 200 miles in the International Belt in London.

Night fell and the hall was emptied of spectators, leaving the walkers and officials alone in the cold and quiet. The *Sporting Life* wrote: 'Slowly the still, chill hours wore away, the peds pursuing their endless rounds under the most depressing circumstances, with no spectators to mark their efforts but the shivering officials, who, cold as charity, and almost too numbed to make a mark, stuck to their figuring till the meagre light of the few gas burners gave way to the scarcely less sickly illumination of a sun striving to make itself visible through rain and fog.' In the half-light and the hush, the sleep-starved walkers' nerves became so strained that the reporter reckoned if someone had shouted 'bogey' they would have stampeded. One of the officials tried to keep off the cold by wrapping up in three coats and a layer of newspaper tied round him with string: 'more miserable work ... can hardly be imagined'.

In the early hours of Wednesday morning, Vaughan dropped out of the race suffering from a sprained ankle. By the time the hall opened its doors to the public again at six, Brown had taken the lead. He and Corkey, both Londoners, spent the day swapping the top two positions. The men were joined for a few laps by an escaped toddler who trotted around drawing cheers and laughter from the pedestrians and from the crowd. During the afternoon, an electric arc light was fitted and was switched on that evening, and the gas lights turned out. London's first electric lights had been installed outside a theatre on the Strand in August but they would not come into widespread use until the 1890s. The *Sporting Life* was not impressed by the innovation: 'No sooner had this fearful invention been started than everyone found it an unmitigated nuisance ... The light was never for a couple of seconds of the same intensity ... After enduring it for a while the effect was that one felt as though the eyes were in fault and not the burner and that some fearful spasmodic affection of the optic nerves and muscles set in.' The 'infernal machine' was switched off and the gas relit at 1 a.m., briefly dazzling the walkers.

By the next day, Thursday 31 October, with three days' walking to go, Weston was more than 40 miles behind the leaders – Corkey, Brown and Crossland – and effectively out of the race, but he was still popular with the crowd. Weston had been entertaining the spectators, playing the clown, only stopping short of turning somersaults, which would have stretched the definition of 'go as you please'.

By Friday, a swollen ankle had put paid to the smallest possibility that Weston might catch the leaders; he retired from the race before evening. Corkey and Brown continued to vie for the lead and were now 40 miles clear of third placed Charles Rowell. The money was on Corkey Gentleman, 'the little wonder' who *Sporting Life* said was 'as honest, plucky and modest as high-born gentlemen can be' and would be 'famous by Monday'. The paper mused that 'as for muscle there is no room for it on him. His bones are hardly covered with flesh, and if he has any digestive organs, they must be stowed somewhere about the back of his head, for his heart is so big it must take up all the space inside his ribs.'

Corkey went to bed before midnight and was back on the track at 2.30 a.m. By 9 a.m. he had put 15 miles between himself and Brown. He cleared 500 miles at lunchtime and just after 7 p.m. finished his 520th and left the track as English Champion. A little later he emerged from his tent for a victory lap, wearing a new yellow and green silk suit, which Sir John Astley had ordered as soon as he saw that Corkey would win. He also ordered a bonnet, 'slightly on the gaudy side', for the winner's wife.

Sir John revealed in his memoir that little Corkey had a secret weapon: 'The winner, Corkey, was a very quaint-looking little old chap, of forty-six ... He didn't look a bit like staying, was as thin as a rail, and stuttered very funnily; but in Mrs Corkey he possessed a real treasure. She never left him day or night and was always ready to hand her sweetheart a basin of delicious and greasy eel-broth, that he loved so well, and which evidently agreed so famously with him.'

The *Sporting Life* declared that the success of this latest long-distance competition confirmed that pedestrianism was a hit, and no flash in the pan either:

> If a fair estimate of the popularity of long-distance competitions may be formed from the numbers of the public who attend them, the tremendous success of the six days' match commenced on Monday last may be fairly reckoned as stamping them as having taken a firm hold at least on the tastes of metropolitan sportsmen. When Weston first came to England and started this form of sport, it was prophesied that after the novelty of the innovation had worn off it would soon die a natural death. It is almost doubtful whether, had not Sir John Astley become a supporter of Weston and taken under his own especial protection what are now known as six days' competitions, that ... we would not have seen the last of these very severe tests of endurance.

Together, Weston and Sir John Astley had established long-distance pedestrianism in Britain. Unfortunately, however, it seemed to have happened just as Weston's star was fading. He had missed the first two International Astley Belt races and limped out of the English Championship. Weston's mother Maria (for whom he kept the sabbath) had died a few months earlier, leaving Edward and his two sisters the only surviving members of his family. And he was in trouble with money again: an American newspaper reported that Weston owed $5,000 and had filed for bankruptcy in England.

Weston had to do something to pay off his debts and get his career back on track. At the start of 1879, he went back to the kind of walking that had made his name – taking to the road. Sir John Astley gave him odds of 5–1 that he could not complete a 2,000-mile route around England in 1,000 hours. The route would take him to 50 towns to deliver 50 lectures on 'What I know about walking'. Weston set off on 18 January, leaving from the Royal Exchange, London, and heading for Folkestone, Kent, his first stop on a tour that would take him all the way west along the south coast to Cornwall, north through Bristol to the West Midlands and on to Cheshire, Lancashire and Cumbria before swinging east across Britain's narrow waist to Newcastle, then south through Yorkshire and East Anglia, then on to the East Midlands and the Home Counties and back to London.

He was accompanied by a group of supporters in a horse-drawn omnibus, but the group's route was beset by troubles: missed roads, tired horses, falls, overenthusiastic fans and bad weather that vividly recalled his previous journeys to Washington and Chicago. He was frequently jostled by crowds of thousands (60,000 met him on the outskirts of

Bolton) and lost time as he struggled to find a path through the hordes. He took to using a carriage to get him in and out of towns or else was given a police escort. He even resorted to the odd train journey in order to keep to his timetable of talks; after all, a missed lecture meant a missed payment. Hundreds and, in some places, thousands paid to hear his thoughts on diet and exercise.

When the thousand hours were up, Weston was between Windsor, his last stop, and London, having walked 1,997 miles. He arrived at the Royal Exchange at midnight, eight hours late. The *New York World* commented: 'The walk as a speculation is said to have been a success, for although his bet of £100 against £500 with Sir John Astley is lost, Weston did so well with his lectures and by the sales of photographs and pamphlets on walking, that it is thought he will clear several hundred pounds.' According to Weston's friends, though, his expenses were so high that he made no money and another failure did nothing to restore his reputation. Weston's decline was not over yet.

THE SECOND LONG DISTANCE CHAMPIONSHIP OF ENGLAND took place at the Agricultural Hall between Monday 21 April and Saturday 26 April 1879. The winner at the end of six days would take all the stake money and half the gate receipts, with smaller shares of the gate money for the others so long as they cleared 450 miles. The contestants were the holder of the belt Corkey Gentleman, George Hazael, Henry 'Blower' Brown and E.P. Weston.

By the Wednesday morning Weston, who had turned 40 a few

weeks before the race, was in last place and complaining of a headache. Sporting Life reported that he looked 'bigger and more muscular' following his weeks tramping the English roads but it did not seem to help him. That evening the scores were: Brown 285 miles; Hazael 276; Corkey 272, Weston 242.

After that the positions never altered, but the telegraph men were kept hard at it changing the scores on the board. Brown had spent three months training for the race on a cinder track laid for him in an orchard in Chiswick, where he was supervised by his wife. His preparation paid off as he gave a wonderful performance, setting new records as he walked, jogged and sprinted his way around and around the hall: 300 miles in 68 hours and 32 minutes; 400 miles in 93 hours and 56 minutes. He had only one hiccup, fainting on the second to last day after running his 455th lap. He was helped to his tent but emerged ten minutes later and, after a few dazed, unsteady laps, was soon back to normal.

Weston, meanwhile, was suffering with painful blisters on his feet but struggled on. He was making a reasonable pace, better than he had managed in any of his recent races, but while Weston stuck to walking the other men mixed running, jogging and walking and left him trailing miles behind.

Brown made his 500th mile at nine o'clock on Saturday morning, with more than 12 hours left of the race. During the remaining hours, Weston rested, Hazael hobbled along on swollen feet and Corkey made slow, stiff progress. Brown floated on in his superhuman orbit, tallying another 42 miles before the match ended at 9.21 p.m. His distance of 542 miles beat Corkey's record by 21 miles. Corkey handed Brown the Challenge Belt in front of a 14,000-strong crowd and news of the record-breaking race was telegraphed to newspapers all over the country.

Weston had finished on 450 miles, enough to secure a share of the takings. He had spent the last day taking it easy and entertaining the audience, knowing that he was out of contention. Weston had brought pedestrianism to Britain. When he first walked in London, people had seen nothing like him; he left his English rivals bloodied and limping while he marched on and on. His achievement seemed wonderful and unbeatable. It was the excitement that Weston created that brought the crowds and the prize money and the silver and gold trophies to pedestrianism, but suddenly it seemed the sport had run away from him. Sir John's decision to make the Astley Belt races 'go as you please' instead of 'heel and toe' had been taken to ensure that Weston's wobbly gait would pass muster, but the change had done for him. Weston was a walker, not a runner, and perhaps he would have to stick to the lecture circuit from now on and leave the prizes to the runners. He and Daniel O'Leary had taken a year or more to break the 500-mile barrier; now this new breed of pedestrian was making leaps of 10 or 20 miles with every new race, and Weston could not keep up.

SO IT SEEMED when the Fourth International Astley Belt was announced, to start on Monday 16 June 1879 at the Agricultural Hall. The Third International Astley Belt had taken place in New York. One of Weston's old competitors, Charles Rowell, had travelled to America to challenge O'Leary, and brought back the belt and $20,000 in winnings.

Weston challenged Rowell for the belt but then had trouble

scraping together the £100 stake he needed to enter the race. After coming last in (or missing) so many races, his standing in the sport had collapsed; the newspapers said his challenge was cheeky. Even Sir John Astley refused to lend him the money, saying that Weston stood no chance, and in the end he borrowed the money from his wife. The starters for the Championship of the World were Blower Brown, John Ennis, Richard Harding and Edward Payson Weston. Charlie Rowell had been put out of the running by injury, and John Ennis's fitness was a cause for concern, too. Sporting Life suspected that a recent 'piece of manliness' might have ruined his chances. Ennis had hurt his back and caught a chill after jumping into the Thames to rescue two ladies whose boat had been hit by a tug.

Brown started the race as odds-on favourite at 4–6; Weston at 10–1 was the outsider. *Sporting Life* suggested that Weston might not be such a bad bet, commenting that 'it is pretty well known that he has been practising getting on his toes lately, and a few good judges are snapping up the tempting odds offered against this indomitable stayer'. When Weston appeared on the track he certainly looked different, dressed in a simple outfit of red worsted tights and a light shirt, but if he was going to win this race he would have to do something far more radical than banishing silk and frills.

The race started in the dark and quiet, at one in the morning, in front of just 100 spectators. Sir John Astley shouted 'Go!' and the pedestrians set off at a fast walking pace. Within a few laps however, the leader Harding started to run and, to everyone's astonishment, so did Weston. By the end of the third hour all four men were running. EPW was in fourth place but by mixing running, walking and trotting he kept pace with the younger men. *Sporting Life* noted a 'vast improvement' in Weston's style, although it was as idiosyncratic as ever, 'a mode of progression peculiar to himself'.

Harding held the lead for two hours, with Brown second, Ennis third and Weston fourth. Harding's success was short-lived, however. By 5 a.m. Brown had taken his lead, Harding was feeling unwell and headed for his tent to rest, and Weston moved up to second place. Harding never regained the lead. At the end of the first day Brown was leading, just, on 131 miles, with Weston on 128; Harding and Ennis had been left far behind on 87 and 70 miles respectively. From then on the race for the Astley Belt became a duel between Brown and Weston.

After a few hours' rest, all four men were back on the track by four o'clock. Brown completed 150 miles just after 8 a.m. on Tuesday. He was leading Weston by seven miles but made up his mind to try and put his rival off his work. Blower Brown's tactic was to 'dog' Weston, sticking to his heels lap after lap. Weston retaliated by altering his pace or changing direction suddenly. According to *Sporting Life*, 'Weston, the old stager, was in no way disconcerted.' In fact 'considerable amusement has been caused by the strict way in which Blower sticks to his principal of dogging Weston, and being with him. Faithful as Mary's Little Lamb, wherever Weston is there Blower goes with him.'

Brown's game made for a dull day however, as the positions on the track hardly altered. Brown was still favourite to win, but it had begun to look like the *Sporting Life* had been right to think Weston might stand a chance, that there might still be life in his career.

Then, suddenly, on Wednesday morning Weston's hopes seemed to fade. Pain and stiffness in his right leg slowed him down and eventually forced him to take a break. Brown increased his lead to 13 miles and by midday was well on his way to his 250th mile. But, just as abruptly, Weston got over the trouble with his leg and picked up speed. Brown made 300 miles at eight o'clock on Wednesday evening, Weston did the same at a quarter past ten, less than 70 hours since the race had started, and was rewarded with an outburst of cheering from the spectators. Weston started to slowly eat away at Brown's lead; his new style of perambulation was working well, even if it looked odd. As *Sporting Life* put it, 'he has swapped wobbling walk for wobbling run and made it pay'.

By Thursday morning Brown was just four miles ahead of the American and was looking unwell. Weston, meanwhile, seemed to be 'in the pink' and was seen to run two miles without stopping. That afternoon, a great shout echoed around the hall: Weston had finally taken the lead and his fans were delighted. Now it was Weston's race: Weston against the clock, as Brown never recovered his lead. In fact, Weston stretched the gap between them to nearly 100 miles before time was up.

This was Weston's chance to prove that pedestrianism was still his sport, even though the rules had changed. Astley made him an offer, or rather a bet: £500 to Weston's £100 if he could do 550 miles by 10.30 on Saturday night. Confident and happy, with resurrection in his sights, Weston set to work. In the last two days of the race, he glided round and round the track, running, walking and jogging, 'as fresh as a lark', his spirits rising further with every lap, mile and world record that fell at his feet.

By 6.30 p.m. on Saturday Weston had made 530 miles. At 9.30 he clocked 542, beating Brown's record by seconds, and announced that he had breath enough to try for 550. The crowd roared their approval and on a track carpeted with flowers thrown from the galleries above Weston picked up his feet and trotted his last eight miles in 85 minutes. As he passed his tent on his last lap, he was handed a British and an American flag and carried them round the ring as the band played 'Yankee Doodle' and 'Rule Britannia'. In 141 hours and 55 minutes, he had walked 550 miles and 110 yards. He was the champion of the world. His redemption was perfect.

The *Boston Globe* reported: 'It may be pertinently said that Edward Payson Weston, the pedestrian, has redeemed himself with a vengeance. He has been heretofore very freely denounced in various quarters as a fraud and a humbug ... He has indeed retrieved his reputation as a pedestrian.' In New York, where the *Herald* news-paper had displayed the cabled bulletins reporting Weston's progress day and night, the city 'yelled itself hoarse in rejoicing over the great American victory'.

Sporting Life added: 'When Weston entered for this journey, the majority thought he would never be 'in it', but there would have seemed something wanting if he had not shown, for, no matter how far he may have been behind on other occasions, he has always put some life into the proceedings. The wonder is how any man, after sticking to walking ... for so many years can have taught himself a new step. It is impossible to describe his run. Nothing like it has ever been seen before, but it plays well enough.' Weston, having originated six-day races, had finally found a way to win them.

WESTON'S TRIUMPH, HOWEVER, did not do much for his pocket. Attendance at this race had been lower than expected, a result of the summer weather which kept Londoners away from indoor entertainment and of the fact that Weston's competitors had faded so soon. Weston made £500 in stake money, the same from his bet with Sir John and £142 as his share of gate receipts. A few days later, Astley organised a testimonial for Weston at the Alexandra Palace to help him out of his 'pecuniary difficulties', the result of the expense of his walking tour and previous 'losses'. He was presented with a gold watch and the profits from ticket sales. But then stories appeared in the American papers alleging that Weston had been involved in a secret betting plot, that a 'well-known wealthy gentleman' had lost $80,000 on Daniel O'Leary in the Third International Belt. Meeting Weston in England, this gentleman was said to have seen a way to recoup his losses, encouraged Weston to go into serious training for the race (and his walk around England was part of this) but to keep it quiet so that the odds against him would remain high. The man was said to have laid $150,000 on Weston, in small bets with most of the sporting chaps in London, and Weston had half of his winnings, perhaps $750,000.

It seems likely this was nothing more than rumour, but it shows how the American press continued to doubt Weston, even while proclaiming him a champion. Plans were being made for the next round of the Astley Belt, and after more than three years in England, Weston was soon on his way back to New York, where he would be forced once again not only to defend his title but his reputation too.

CHAPTER *12*

5,000

OYSTERS,

5,000 PIGS'

TROTTERS

ON WEDNESDAY 27 AUGUST 1879, thousands of New Yorkers gathered at the gates of Manhattan's Pier 38 to await the arrival of a steamship, the Nevada, which had been delayed a day by fog and headwinds. As a ship finally approached and a figure appeared at the side rail, a great cheer flew into the air; when the man lifted a leather case containing the famous Astley Belt he set off a new storm of applause.

Weston had been in England for three and a half years. According to the *Chicago Tribune*, he looked years younger than he had when he left the States with a trail of humiliating defeats behind him: 'His face was smooth, giving him an almost boyish appearance, and the only indication of advancing age were the few gray hairs about his temples.' Weston was pleased with his success but seemed to find it hard to forgive the doubt and hostility that had been his lot when he left the USA and which he knew he would face on his return. In fact, he had wanted to go to Australia instead of home, but his wife and Sir John Astley changed his mind. He told journalists: 'Actions speak louder than words; but there is nothing succeeds like success, gentlemen. I have seen the time in this city when I could not borrow $25 to keep the rink open another day when I was walking ... There was a time when I would have considered it the proudest event of my life to bring this belt back to America, but I have got over that. Still, I am glad to bring it back for the sake of my friends.'

This triumphant return to New York, with the International Astley Belt in his hands, was the high point of Weston's career although, at the age of 40, he was a long way yet from hanging up his walking boots, especially following his euphoric discovery that he could run as well as he could walk. He told reporters:

While I was in this country I never believed that running could hold out against walking, but when I saw the easy pace of some of those runners, I changed my mind. Some of the men ran a ten-mile gait with less apparent exertion than a man makes walking four miles an hour.

... As to the running, I like it. I fell accidentally into an easy running race, just as I did in walking. I never ran a mile in my life till a month before the last London race. I hardly knew I could run. Dr Newman, of New York, preached a sermon about the 'brutality' of walking matches. I have walked 53,000 miles in the last 14 years, and I don't look much like a used-up man, do I?

As his coach trundled out through the pier gates towards the Rossmore Hotel on Broadway, the crowd pressed around the coach with more cheers, trying to catch another glimpse of the famous pedestrian and his wife and children. A party for Weston, a reception at Madison Square Garden that evening, was attended by 6,000 men and women.

THOUSANDS OF BOATS LOADED WITH PASSENGERS and goods landed every day at a hundred-odd piers and wharves that frayed the edge of Manhattan Island. The same day that Weston landed on the Nevada, Charles Rowell stepped off the Bothnia, and two days later Blower Brown arrived on the California at Pier 21. George Hazael landed with the Montana on 9 September. John Ennis had arrived on board the City of Berlin in July. With Dan O'Leary in town busy manufacturing his own pedestrian empire with the Daniel O'Leary Belt, the picture was complete. As the *Chicago Tribune* said, the walkers were about to make America crazy again.

The occasion was the Fifth International Astley Belt, Rowell and Hazael having challenged Weston for the title almost as soon as he won it. Weston agreed to defend the Belt at the Madison Square Garden on one condition: he wanted smoking banned from the building during the race. At his reception in the Garden in August, he had addressed a comment to the 'young men of this City': 'If you will abstain from smoking in this building during the next match, you will see one of the greatest pedestrian contests ever attempted in the world.' He also told them that they could walk and run as far and as fast as he did, if they lived like he did, including not smoking. Weston's demand was admitted: 'no smoking' signs would be put up in the Garden, quite an unusual sight in the 19th century.

The race was to start on Monday 22 September, but there were a few hiccups before then. For one thing, Daniel O'Leary was stirring up trouble and delayed arrangements. Since returning from London, O'Leary had taken part in a few races in New York, but had either lost or quit all of them. According to the newspapers, Dan, always fond of an ale or a glass of champagne, was now 'on a protracted spree' and was drinking on and off the track. The *Chicago Tribune* called him 'a pitiful wreck', but in fact O'Leary was not in such a poor state. While he had given up on walking himself, he was dabbling in promotion instead, and had organised a competition of his own. He had booked the same venue for a race in October and he was not happy for the Astley Belt race to take place in September. He did not want Astley stealing his thunder or indeed his walkers, as the most famous pedestrians were not interested in taking part in two long races so close together.

O'Leary appealed to the owner of the Garden, the Vanderbilt family. Cornelius Vanderbilt asked Astley to postpone his race until October. Astley refused to postpone but managed to hush O'Leary's objections by paying him off. Further delay was caused by arguments and accusations between the American and English parties, the Americans claiming that they were being shut out of the organisation of ticket sales and contract agreements so that the English (which here included Weston) could tie up the profits between them. The event was to be managed by an opera impresario called Charles Hess who had recently sold his touring English Opera Company and seemed to be between ventures.

On Saturday 20 September, preparations began. During the afternoon, carpenters laid a wooden floor for the spectators and built stout rails to keep them off the arena. In the evening, 100 labourers arrived to dig, rake and roll the track itself. Tents were pitched for the competitors, blue and white striped for all except Weston, who had yellow and black. Each tent was furnished with a bed, table, washstand, chairs, stove and carpet.

The 'no smoking' signs were up and electric lights installed and fitted with shades to soften the light. There were cake stands, apple carts, weighing machines, soda fountains and an extra bar to help part the audience from their dollars. Entrance was set at $1 — to 'keep the worst sort out' — and the building shut to spectators during the depths of night to stop it turning into a boarding house.

By seven o'clock in the evening of Sunday 21st, hundreds of people had gathered in the streets around the building to wait for the doors to open. There were 100 police on duty throughout the event, 20 stationed at each entrance when the doors finally opened at 10 p.m. During the next two hours, 13,000 people paid their dollar and filed into the Garden to see the 13 competitors line up for the start of the six-day race.

Rowell, the winner of the last Astley Belt match to take place in America, was favourite to win, followed by Weston, with George Hazael third. John Ennis, the best known of the remaining ten competitors, was ranked seventh after Frank Hart, a protégé of O'Leary and the only black contestant for the title. The other pedestrians who had paid the $500 deposit to take part comprised seven Americans — George Guyon, Frederick Krohne, a German-born New Yorker Peter Panchot, Samuel Merritt, William Dutcher, Hiram Jackson and Norman Taylor — and a long-haired Frenchman from Lorraine called Leon Federmeyer.

The race began at 1 a.m. exactly on Monday 22 September. The event was a startling commercial success and the audience had a whale of a time. Attendance started high and remained so for the six days. By the end, the bartenders, officials and musicians were almost as exhausted as the pedestrians. Over the week, the lunch room sold thousands of sandwiches made from 400 loaves of bread, as well as 5,000 pigs' trotters, 5,000 oysters, 6,000 pickled sheep's tongues, 100lb of roast beef and two barrels of eggs. Gallons of clam chowder were sold, along with 200,000 glasses of lager and 8,000 bottles of soda.

From morning till night, the band kept up a parade of popular songs including 'Pop Goes the Weasel', as well as numbers from the Gilbert and Sullivan show HMS Pinafore, which had opened in London the year before and was about to have its first official opening in New York. During Friday night, the final night of walking, the Garden remained open and more than 1,000 people stayed. According to the *Brooklyn Eagle*, those that did were a mixed crowd: 'There were women there whose bleached hair, cheeks flushed with rouge, gaudy costumes, and "loud" manner showed them to be fast; there were gamblers with big diamonds and dyed moustaches, and there were dwellers in the lower strata of society; but these collectively only formed a minority of the crowd, for with them sat hundreds of respectable people, intent on seeing every feature of the great walk.'

Local florists had a bumper week, as each day some local business or chamber of commerce advertised itself by having a giant floral ship, anchor or cross delivered to one of the athletes. Weston, however, received nothing. He did badly even on the first day. The 'no smoking' signs were worthless; at one point, according to the papers, the fog of smoke that hung over the track made it impossible to see from one side of the oval to the other. Weston divided his time on the track between complaining about the smoke and playing up to the audience. He made the occasional spurt, running a mile inside six minutes during the third day, but dropped steadily back in the field until he was 70 miles behind the leaders, Rowell, Merritt and Hazael. Meanwhile, he acted the fool, knocking a judge's hat off, skipping across the track, and impersonating the other walkers.

By the final two days, the crowd had tired of his antics and apparently so had Weston. According to one report:

> *Weston was a thorough disappointment to his friends and a laughing stock early in the week to the spectators who jeered him for his buffoonery. Later, when the old ex-champion went along the track with a pinched face, unsteady gait and straining eyes, the picture of a broken down and miserable man, the people remained silent, realizing that he had broken down utterly, bodily and mentally. The sight was pitiable, and the silence of the crowd as he passed by alternately laughing and crying deepened the sadness of the scene.*

The race was won by the Cambridge man Charles Rowell, who ended on 530 miles, 20 short of Weston's record, at 8 p.m., with five hours left on the clock. Maria was there to see Weston end the race on 455 miles and together they hurried away from the Garden to their hotel. Later, Weston told journalists that he had not been in condition for the match, that he had been upset by the deaths of several dear friends and that of his mother. His 'buffoonery', he said, was to distract himself from walking and losing and he insisted he had not intended to 'trifle with the people'.

Weston's comeback had been glorious but brief. Just a few weeks after sailing into New York in triumph, with the Astley Belt in his hand, he had lost both the prize and the respect that he had worked so hard, and for so long, to win.

CHAPTER

TEA

VERSUS

BEER

IN THE 1880S, PEDESTRIANISM REACHED THE HEIGHT OF ITS FAME and popularity; there were two new major competitions, the American Rose Belt and the Daniel O'Leary Belt, as well as scores of smaller events taking place on both sides of the Atlantic and more competitions in New Zealand and Australia. Charles Rowell and Frank Hart dominated the major events, while Weston had gone into temporary retirement following his tearful failure in the Fifth Astley International race. O'Leary was concentrating on promoting his championship. In London in November 1880, Rowell won the Sixth International Astley Belt; if he won again, he would become the permanent owner of the gold and silver belt.

Weston had missed that race and it looked as though, at the age of 41, he had gone into retirement. Then in March 1881, he decided on one more throw of the dice and challenged Rowell for the Belt. The race, which would take place in London, was expected to have just three entrants: Weston, Rowell and Frank Hart. In an unexpected twist, on 4 June, Hart appeared in court charged with assaulting a French woman and stealing 25 shillings from her. He was committed for a trial at Middlesex Court of Sessions and, although released on bail, he withdrew from the race.

The match started at the Marble Rink in Clapham on Monday 20 June with just two competitors, Weston and Rowell. Hart and Daniel O'Leary were among many Americans in the audience. Weston's challenge did not hold up long as he became ill on the first day. He recovered during the second day, but by then Rowell was leading by more than 60 miles. Weston had no hope of catching the Cambridge man and ceded the race, and the Belt, on the third afternoon, having walked 201 miles.

Edward and Maria had travelled back to England by themselves, but in 1882 Maria sailed back across the ocean to collect Lillian and the younger children and bring them to Europe to be with their parents. Weston's career plans had taken a new turn. Through his contacts with various London doctors, Weston had become involved with the British temperance movement; he was offered $10,000 to become an ambassador for temperance, taking a message of 'tea versus beer' on a 5,000-mile walking tour of England.

The tour would keep Weston and his family in Europe until at least 1884, and at first 19-year-old Lillian was delighted to have the chance to spend time in London. She enjoyed the city's concerts and art galleries but was frustrated by the education that was offered to well-to-do young English ladies. Lillian later complained that much of her school day was spent learning to curtsy and wrote that: 'the height of each student's ambition was to be presented at the Court of St James'. Edward and Maria sent Lillian to the best school they could afford, but as the daughter of an athlete, and an American one at that, Lillian was snubbed by her teachers and by the other girls. Her major consolation was in attending the London Academy of Music to study piano.

Despite this, Lillian grew so unhappy with her London life that she begged her parents to send her to Paris. They refused to allow her to live in a boarding house by herself in the city but eventually agreed to send her to a convent school on Rue Monceau in the eighth arrondissement. After a few months, when she could stand the cold and silence of the convent no longer, she moved out to a boarding house run by an American acquaintance of her parents. It was a shabby building on a dingy street, but the sheets were clean and Lillian made the best of it, attending lectures at the Sorbonne and the Collège de France.

With Lillian in Paris and the other children in Brighton with Maria, Edward began his walking tour of England in November 1883. He was to walk 50 miles a day for 100 consecutive days, excluding Sundays and Christmas Day. A route had been planned for him by the Ordnance Survey Department and every evening he would deliver a lecture on temperance and exercise or in church halls and college buildings.

Weston's route began in London and took him on a looping, winding path around cities and towns. He would walk the roads in the daytime in snow, fog and blinding rain, then make up his 50 miles at a rink or hall before he gave his talk in the evening. Of his 5,000 miles, 3,000 were walked on England's cold and muddy roads. His last call was at the Royal Victoria Coffee House, London (now the Old Vic theatre). Mounted police had accompanied him from Croydon to protect him from the crowd that followed to see him finish. In the first week of his marathon, an injury to his foot had apparently become infected and doctors in Oxford had tried to stop him from continuing the walk, but Weston had pressed on (he said there was $10,000 at stake) and finished his 5,000th mile in good time. When he saw Sir John Astley, he told him that on his seventieth birthday he would walk across America.

WESTON DID NOT WALK AGAIN ALL THAT YEAR and his family left England for the last time in the summer of 1885 to return to New York. Parts of another famous American steamed into NYC that summer: the remaining pieces of the Statue of Liberty (one arm and leg had been on display in the city for some years) arrived packed in crates on a boat called the Isere and were met by hundreds of thousands of New Yorkers.

The arrival of the Weston family was far less auspicious. On reaching America, their ship was held in quarantine because two of her passengers, immigrants travelling in steerage, were suffering from smallpox. At least two other transatlantic steamers had small-pox on board that summer, and an epidemic in Montreal was thought to have been started by a steamship passenger. There were thousands of cases in European cities, including London, and the authorities in New York were wary of inadvertently letting the virus migrate to their city. The sick passengers were transferred to a quarantine hospital on Ward Island in the East River and the rest were vaccinated and held on board for days while the ship and their baggage were fumigated.

New York escaped. Occasional, isolated cases emerged that summer, but health officers acted quickly to disinfect their homes and to vaccinate their relatives. A few years later Lillian wrote of her fear at 'being imprisoned on the ship with the dread disease' and of her sadness at being in sight of home but out of touch: 'Whenever I hear a buoy bell, I feel like crying ... I never forgot standing at the rail looking at land but not being allowed to put a foot on it.'

A few months after the Weston family landed, Edward was back on the road, walking against his old rival Daniel O'Leary. While Weston had been on his second stay in England, O'Leary had been in Sydney, Australia, where he lost three races to an English-born New Zealander called William Edwards. He had written to a Melbourne newspaper claiming that during their first race Edwards' backers had spiked his drinking water with ether. However, while Edwards had a reputation for chicanery, as O'Leary also lost the next two races it seems more likely that Dan was spiking his own drinks.

Weston and O'Leary, now aged 47 and 39 respectively, had met at the office of *Turf, Field and Farm* magazine in New York and signed an agreement to race each other in a peripatetic event over 2,500 miles, walking 12 hours a day (but not Sundays) in numerous locations until the distance was done. The challenge was sponsored by a New York temperance campaigner, who offered a purse of $3,000 plus the net gate receipts (the winner getting two-thirds of both sums, the loser the remaining third), and the men had agreed to walk only in rinks and halls where alcohol was not served. The temperance movement had been building since the beginning of the century and in 1870 the Prohibition Party had run its first election campaign. The party scored only a couple of thousand votes that year, but by the 1880s momentum was gathering and the party collected towards 150,000 votes in the 1884 election. It would still be more than 30 years before the campaigners succeeded in having prohibition written into the constitution in the 18th Amendment.

While Weston had been advocating moderation for years, taking money from the temperance movement seems an odd move for Daniel O'Leary. He was far from being an obvious poster boy for healthy consumption, but was in good form when the race started at the Metropolitan Rink in Newark, New Jersey, on Monday 7 December 1885. Dressed in a tightly buttoned winter sack coat, white tights and light lace-up shoes, he whisked round the first few laps at a speed of five miles per hour, working 'like a piece of machinery'. Weston took his time to start with, lingering to chat with the band and newspapermen. 'I haven't walked since March 1884 in England and then I covered 5,000 miles,' he told them. 'O'Leary has always beaten me and he says he can again on a long trip. Now I don't think so. I propose to give his boast a practical test.'

The men spent the rest of the first week of the challenge in Newark, pacing from 10.30 a.m. to 10.30 p.m. each day round the outside edge of the rink while in the middle women and children skated and listened to the band playing. A newspaper reported that Weston had the end of a toe knocked off in a collision with a roller skater.

By the first Saturday, O'Leary was ahead on 284 miles to Weston's 234, and won $300 for leading at the end of the first week. That Sunday the two men travelled to New Brunswick, New Jersey. They spent the second week in New Jersey and the third, including Christmas, walking the days away at the Cosmopolitan Skating Rink in New York. O'Leary still held on to his lead, though Weston had managed to cut it to 20 miles.

At their next destination, Erie, Pennsylvania, now in the middle of January 1886, O'Leary began to show signs that all was not well. On Wednesday 20th, he started to abuse Weston, shouting at him, and then pushed him off the track. By the 44th day of walking, the men had walked 2,067 miles and 2,058 miles, with O'Leary leading now by just nine miles. A few days later they were on their way to Chicago, having already passed through Cleveland and Cincinnati. Then, on Thursday 4 February, Weston was walking alone: Daniel O'Leary had failed to show up. Weston was declared the winner of the contest and went on to complete 2,500 miles on Saturday 6 February.

The next day, a journalist with the *Rochester Democrat and Chronicle* bumped into Weston at Rochester train station. Weston, who now had a silvery beard and moustache, gave the reporter his explanation for O'Leary's failure: 'You see, about a week before we finished the contest, Dan commenced to take stimulants pretty freely. I don't mean that he went on a spree. But the fact is that he was so exhausted that whisky was the only thing which would keep him up. Food had no effect on him ... It will be some time before he will be able to do much walking.' He later said that O'Leary should have consumed something other than Jersey lightning (a concentrated cider) if he had wanted to win the race.

CHAPTER 14

THE

SHACKLES

THEY BOTH

HATED

IN THE SPRING OF 1886, Weston announced that he was retiring from pedestrianism after a 25-year career in which he reckoned to have walked 62,000 miles. He made the announcement at a testimonial in Rochester, New York State, a week after his final triumph over O'Leary. After regaling the audience with his 'celebrated lecture', 'The Advantages of Temperance in Connection with Athletic Exercises', Weston said: 'I have made up my mind that I have done enough walking in my time, and now I prefer to tell others in my humble way, how to walk.'

Putting competitive walking behind him, for now at least, Weston began to see himself as a public figure, an authority on good health. In England in 1882, he had worked with the army temperance movement at the Soldiers Institute in Portsmouth, one of numerous alcohol-free rest homes which aimed to address the problem of excessive drinking in the lower ranks. While Weston was keen on temperance, he made it clear in his lecture in Rochester that he was no prohibitionist, saying, 'I don't believe in total abstinence, but I do believe in temperance. I can't take the ground that this country is going to the devil because the total abstinence people can't have their way. I will say this, however, that you can't make people sober with acts of legislature. You must get at their hearts.' Weston's brand of temperance was more of a 'little of what you fancy' approach; everything was permissible if it was part of a healthy lifestyle, including lots of exercise.

Weston often said that walking was the very best kind of exercise and recommended walking to young men if they wanted to be fit. Now, back in America, he organised a committee of the great and the good to help him put his beliefs into action. His team included decorated Civil War veterans as well as doctors, police commissioners, politicians, prominent writers and religious leaders.

At the beginning of June, the *New York Times* announced that Weston was mounting 'a grand military test of physical endurance'. A businessman and former Congressman John H. Starin had agreed to host the competition at his Glen Island resort, a cluster of five islands in Long Island Sound which Starin had made into a destination for New York's middle classes. Each summer thousands of New Yorkers arrived by steamboat to enjoy the sea air and bathing beaches and to visit the zoo, museum, castle and beer garden which were scattered among the islands' trees. A few years later, Lillian Weston visited Glen Island and wrote about it in one of her newspaper columns. She liked the scenery but was less impressed by the class of visitors: 'It is not a very aristocratic resort ... but I enjoy mingling with the common herd and it is such a delightful place.'

With the title of the 'Military Camp in Instructions in Marching', Weston's project was an international summer camp for volunteer national guards and he personally supervised the installation of a training camp and walking track, as well as tents to house the soldiers. Each week for nine weeks, groups of volunteer guards would take part in walking competitions, walking for 66 hours over six days in 'heavy marching order', carrying knapsack, rifle and equipment weighing more than 40lb, 'as they would be required to be were they in the field, making a forced march. This test would give some idea of the value of the country's national guard for active service.' The camp would end with a contest between volunteers from the United States, Canada and Britain.

Saturday 21 June was the grand launch day of the camp. The *New York Times* reported that numerous prominent public figures rubbed shoulders with the volunteer guards and 'a sprinkling of sisters, cousins and aunts who all came up on the Sam Sloan [steamer] amid the clashing of cymbals and the sounding of drums'. Seated among the trees of Glenwood Grove were a prominent New York rabbi, Gustav Gottheil; the founder of the American Society for the Prevention of Cruelty to Animals, Henry Bergh, who was also influential in the creation of the American Society for the Prevention of Cruelty to Children and had been appointed by Lincoln to the American legation in Russia in 1862; and theatre producer and future movie maker Gustave Frohman.

Proceedings were begun by Weston's old friend from his New York walks in the early 1870s, Dr Ogden Doremus: 'We are indebted to Mr Weston as the father of walking. I have positively been asked to make a chemical analysis of him to see how he did it. Since 1867, he has walked 63,500 miles and Dr Richardson, who examined him in London, said he was the healthiest man he had ever examined. I would advise all, if they desire good health, to sweat daily as the result of physical exercise.

Gentlemen, I look upon this camp as the initiative step towards splendid results in this country.' According to the *Times*' mischievous reporter, Weston's 'moustache twitched bashfully' as he paced up and down the grove 'either to show that he still retained the art of pedestrianism or to reveal his brand new trousers'.

This seemed like the grand overture to an illustrious new career for Weston, as an expert adviser mending the health of the nation, but the commotion quickly faded and for some reason, the results of Weston's military exercise were never reported. Perhaps the public lost interest or perhaps he did; nothing ever held Weston's attention like actually getting out and walking himself.

BY THE FOLLOWING SUMMER he seemed to be content to enjoy his retirement. A reporter for a Philadelphia newspaper visited him at his home in Highbridge, a neighbourhood of the Bronx. The journalist sat with Weston on his porch eating cherries. He wrote: 'His hair is dashed with white, but he is in splendid condition with a ruby glow on his cheeks and the light of health in his eyes. He still walks everywhere, no matter how far along the streets he may have to go, because he says the street cars are too slow for him.' Weston told his visitor, that 'pedestrianism has netted me about $80,000 in savings, but I am done with it because it has lost its tone and become loafery. I mounted the ladder of that sport to its utmost height when I walked in England for the Church of England Temperance Society, and, realising that there were no more rungs to ascend, I quit the turf.'

But, while Weston was enjoying the peace of the Bronx, other pedestrians were finding new rungs to climb. Since Edward's amazing comeback in the Fourth Astley Belt race in London in 1879, when he had set a new record of 550 miles in six days, that number had been getting larger and larger. Just a year later, Frank Hart had made the first big jump, raising the figure to 565 miles. Then in 1882, George Hazael became the first to cover 600 miles in six days; in 1888 another Englishman, George Littlewood, set a record that would remain unbroken for 96 years: 623 miles in six days. Yiannis Kouros, a Greek ultra-marathon runner, finally surpassed Littlewood's achievement in 1984, running 635 miles, though he didn't do it in tights, leather boots and knickerbockers, or in a smoky hall with a boisterous crowd wandering onto the track.

Meanwhile, Weston stuck to his porch and maintained that pedestrianism was not the sport it had been. In the spring of 1891, in an interview with the Philadelphia Ledger, he said: 'I tried to elevate the sport. There is no exercise like walking, and I attribute my present health and vigour to the walking I have done. It is a pity that the contests cannot be conducted on the elevated plane they once were.'

A small paragraph in the *New York Times* in the same year suggested that Weston was continuing to pursue a life outside sport and was still cutting a dash in New York:

> One of the unique figures down town is a well-built, energetic
> man of medium stature and traces of gray in his hair. He flits
> briskly in and out of banks, brokers' offices and lawyers'
> libraries. A quarter of a century ago, he was the most noted

pedestrian in the world. He still retains some of his old grace and elasticity, which serve him admirably in his present modest calling of general solicitor and collector. He performed a prominent part in the raising of the money for the Washington memorial arch.

However, Weston's happy retirement did not last long. In 1893, changes in his home life and in the economy conspired to get him back on the road. The 1880s had been a wonderfully prosperous decade. New industrial processes, a sprawling railroad network and a leapfrogging population meant that America could make more of everything faster than ever before. 1890 was a watershed year: the war with the Native Americans ended with the Battle of Wounded Knee, Oklahoma was opened to settlement, the last frontier crossed. Then 1893 brought a new panic and the start of another new depression.

That tricky year was also when Edward's marriage to Maria finally ended. The family story is that the couple quarrelled about Ellsworth, their only son. Edward and Ellsworth did not get on (Lillian did not appear to like him much either), and Weston told the boy to leave his house. Maria protested and Edward was the one to leave instead. Edward and Maria's great-granddaughter Joyce Litz has written that their separation was no surprise, that family gossip suggested Weston was a bit of a womaniser (he certainly never discouraged the various ladies who pressed kisses on him when he was young and famous) and that the final argument was the culmination of years of unhappiness on both sides. Lillian described their marriage as 'the shackles they both hated', and it is telling that when Lillian thought about her own future, she viewed marriage as 'the end of everything'.

The saddest part of the story is that Lillian never saw her father again. What she knew of his life afterwards, she knew from the newspapers; although she does not say so, a magazine article she wrote about her father in 1928 relied heavily on newspaper cuttings for information about his foibles and habits in his later life. When later he had his last comeback, she never admitted to anyone in her Montana community that the amazing 70-year-old man walking to San Francisco and back was her father.

Although he was no longer living with Maria and the children, all now in their twenties but still dependent, Weston supported them financially. With two households to run now, perhaps his $80,000 savings were disappearing a little faster than he liked. At the end of the year he left Maria and in December 1893, 54-year-old Weston took up walking once again.

He had a new hobby horse too. Having already tackled drinking and smoking, his new project was the working-class diet, which in his view was too meaty. His plan was to walk from New York City to Albany, New York State, a distance of around 150 miles, in three days in order to 'show the poorer working classes the utter absurdity of the belief that hard labour can not be done except on a meat diet'.

He set off from Bowling Green Park at the foot of Broadway at 9 p.m. on Monday 18 December. He was to be followed to Albany by his doctor and the judges travelling in a carriage while a 'tally-ho' (a coach with four horses reined to one driver) filled with members of the New York press club kept him company as far as the edge of the city. Setting off, he was tailed by 'an army of urchins' and '800 young men interested in walking and like sports'. As the procession moved north to the higher reaches of Broadway, nearer to the shops, more and more 'boys and girls and men and women [followed] him with all the apparent interest in the walker that the crowds used to show him in the days when he walked in the American Institute and Madison Square Garden with the other professional pedestrians'.

Walking day and night on icy roads, Weston arrived in Albany at 9.40 a.m. on Thursday 21 December, more than 11 hours ahead of time, and by afternoon had recovered enough to catch a train back to New York city. The next day, the *Brooklyn Eagle* printed a notice which clarified just why Weston had suddenly become interested in working-class eating habits:

> *Edward Payson Weston says: 'In my recent walk from New York to Albany, 150 miles in 60 hours, I subsisted entirely on H-O Oatmeal and H-O Crackers without any flesh food or stimulant of any kind, and I personally selected H-O Oatmeal because of its nutritious and digestible qualities.'*

Lucky Weston had found himself a sponsor just when he needed money to help him keep his two households going in hard economic times.

His next walk was for a wager of $1,000 made by a John Chamberlain (possibly John E. Chamberlain, a Vermont Republican politician). In less than 12 days in the autumn of 1894, Weston hiked 468 miles around the eastern half of New York State, starting and finishing in Newburgh and taking in numerous towns and villages en route. At stops on the way, Weston spoke for the Republican candidates for the New York State elections.

A few months later, the *Buffalo Express* reported: 'John Chamberlain of Washington has offered to bet that Edward Payson Weston can walk from San Francisco to New York in 100 days, and cover a distance of between 3,500 and 3,800 miles.' Weston would only make $2,500 from the bet, not enough to cover both his expenses and those of the judges who would have to accompany him by coach. He had talked before of walking across the continent, 20 years ago, and had been dismissed by the newspapers as a humbug. And, though nothing came of it this time either, the idea was reborn in Weston's mind; even now in middle age Weston dreamed of walking to the Pacific shore.

CHAPTER *15*

WITHOUT

SACRED

VOWS OR

LEGAL BOND

FOR THREE YEARS, Weston supported Maria and their grown-up children. At some point during that time, he fell in love with a young woman called Annie O'Hagan, who would be by his side for the rest of his life. In 1896, Edward asked Maria for a divorce so that he could marry Annie, but Maria refused; Weston told her that she would not have another cent of support from him.

Unable to marry, Edward and Annie lived together for years; where Annie is referred to in the newspapers she is described as his secretary, his housekeeper, his niece or even his adopted daughter. There would have been a scandal if the couple had admitted to 'living in sin' (and goodness knows what Weston's mother would have thought), but of course Ed's family knew the truth. Lillian felt sorry for her mother, but sympathised with her father too and felt that he had met someone who truly loved him. Many years later, according to Joyce Litz, she told her mother: 'She didn't steal your husband. She didn't even meet Dad until you and he had been separated three years. That was twenty years ago and all this time she has lived with him and made him happy without sacred vows or legal bonds. I'll tell the world I take my hat off to her.' She described Annie as 'the woman who gave everything to my father and stood by him through thick and thin'. According to Lillian, Annie had come from a respectable family and gave up her home and her reputation to be with Edward.

By the time of Lillian's conversation with her mother, she had been married for more than 20 years herself and knew a bit about standing by her man. Lillian met Frank Hazen in 1890 when she was 25 and making a little money as a journalist, writing a column called 'Lillian's Letter' which was syndicated in local newspapers in Connecticut, Montana and Virginia. 'Lillian's Letter' gave its readers a taste of New York life; she wrote about fashion and the theatre as well as, occasionally, the darker side of city life, the poverty and squalor.

At first, Frank's parents fiercely opposed the marriage. The Hazens did not want their son to marry an athlete's daughter; at one time he told her that he could not ask her to marry him because 'if I should marry against [my father's] wishes, my wife and I would be beggars'. Frank was in business with his father, buying Boston apartment houses on loans and renting them out, and he could not afford to defy him.

Something must have changed the Hazens' mind, however, because in 1895, two years after Weston had left the family, Frank finally asked Lillian to marry him. Perhaps the fact that Lillian no longer saw her disreputable parent helped to smooth things over with the family. But Lillian's happiness did not last long. She soon realised that she and Frank were every bit as ill-matched as Edward and Maria had been. Frank was obsessively tidy, Lillian was disorganised; Frank was uptight and prone to silences, Lillian was expressive and lively. Worse was to come. Within two years of the wedding, the Hazens lost their money and their business. Little more than a year after Lillian and Frank's first baby, Barbara, arrived in August 1896, the new family were forced to move from their large rented home into a cheap boarding house, selling their wedding gifts to pay the rent.

WHILE GROWN-UP, married life was trying his daughter's strength, Weston's new life with Annie seemed to take him, briefly, back to his youth. In 1896 he decided to try to repeat one of his great feats of more than 20 years before. In May 1874 he had walked 112 miles in 24 hours; on Chistmas night 1896, at the Palace skating rink on Lexington Avenue, New York City, Weston would try to repeat that triumph – perhaps it would be the start of a proper comeback, a return to the top of pedestrian racing.

According to a newspaper report, the walk had been proposed by a group of his friends, doctors and army veterans whom he had known since the height of his fame in the 1870s. Weston wrote in response to their invitation:

> When I was walking, my purpose was to demonstrate that the greatest physical endurance is possible without the use of alcoholic or other artificial stimulants ... On a strictly temperance diet I repeatedly accomplished feats of endurance which no athlete using stimulants has ever equaled. But I am now, as you are well aware, well into the 'sear and yellow leaf' period of my life.

It is nearly a quarter of a century since I made a public
display of what powers I possessed. Still, thanks to my devotion
to the great cause of temperance, I am still hearty and robust, so
I therefore cheerfully accept your kind invitation.

As well as his committee of friends, Weston had the backing of the President of the Board of New York Police Commissioners, Theodore Roosevelt, who had written a letter promising to start the race. But not everyone shared the future President of America's confidence in Weston. Newspaper reports said that Weston was 30lb heavier than he had been in his heyday and some journalists reckoned that at the age of 57 he was foolish to even attempt the feat. Weston countered that he would do the 112 miles in less than 24 hours. At 10 p.m. on Christmas evening, with Commissioner Roosevelt delayed by work, a young woman was picked from the crowd to shout 'Go!'

Dressed in knickerbockers, leggings, cape and yachting cap, Weston got away well and covered the first ten miles in less than two hours. By half-past eight on Boxing Day morning he had finished the first 50 miles. Through the morning, skaters arrived to use the rink and some kept pace with him as he circled the ice. By midday he had walked a few laps more than 65 miles and was on target to finish 115 miles by the end of the day. At 1 p.m., on 70 miles, he stopped for the first time to change his clothes and tuck into eggs, calf's foot jelly and beef tea (but no H-O oats or crackers).

After half an hour Weston was back on the track, clocking 82 miles by 4 p.m. and keeping on walking 'like a well-regulated machine'. Everything seemed to be going to Weston's plan, he was walking as quickly and comfortably as he had done in his twenties and thirties. Then, disaster struck. Up to that point, Weston had had no more than 30 minutes rest and at around 5.15 p.m. he became dizzy and had to be helped from the track 'as weak as a baby'. Less than an hour later he was on his feet again and, spurred on by the cheering crowd, he took his total to 90 miles by 6.39 p.m. Then, again suffering from dizziness, he was forced to take another rest and by the time he returned to the track 25 minutes later he had fallen seven miles behind schedule. At 9.06 p.m. he had scored 98 miles; with just 54 minutes' walking time left and 14 miles to do, Weston realised the task was impossible.

According to a newspaper report, 'he seemed much downcast and he left the track and for a few moments sat in one of the boxes, so over-come by regret that he burst into tears'. Weston's doctor comforted him and he returned to the track, but staggered off again at 9.56 p.m. having completed 103 miles, nine short. Weston's friends gathered around to try to console him, but Edward would not be comforted. He said, 'I am a fool, and had better sell out. Just think of it. I have only walked at that rate of four miles an hour. A mule could do better than that. I have covered a greater distance than 112 miles in 24 hours many a time, and the thought that I have failed now to do so almost breaks my heart.'

Weston never took part in a track race again. For years he stayed out of view while he recovered from the blow to his vanity and his hopes for a comeback. By the time he re-emerged into public life, it would be a new century. In the intervening years, the last few of the 19th century, the worst depression America had ever experienced eventually came to an end, but two of Weston's children were struggling.

IN JULY 1898, LILLIAN AND FRANK'S son Richard was born, another mouth
to feed. The following year brought good news, but also upheaval, as
Frank got the chance of a job as an accountant with the Great Northern
Mining and Development Company out in Montana. With something
of her father's great optimism, Lillian wrote in a letter to Frank: 'I
look forward to being far from the madding crowd, and anyway, it
sounds as if every man has a chance to strike it rich.' Lillian and Frank's
difficulties, however, were far from over.

At the same time, Ellsworth, the son who had apparently been the
final impetus behind Weston's split from Maria, was in terrible trouble.
In November 1898 the Brooklyn Eagle reported that Ellsworth Weston,
'son of the famous pedestrian', had attempted suicide, shooting himself
in the ear and the forehead at the office in Manhattan where he worked
as a clerk to the estate of former Secretary of State, Hamilton Fish. The
paper stated that Ellsworth's work was in order but reported that he had
separated from his wife Mary, the mother of his two young children,
and moved back in with his mother. The young man's doctor said that a
bullet had penetrated to the base of his brain, that 'no operation could
save him' and he might not live till morning. Mary and Maria sat all
night at Ellsworth's bedside, his wife 'weeping bitterly'. There is no
mention of his father attending the hospital. But Ellsworth survived the
night and recovered from his injuries. In 1902, Mary divorced him and
was granted custody of their children.

Also in 1902, Edward Weston reappeared in the New York
papers. In February, a 'go as you please' race took place in Madison

Square Garden and Weston was there, not competing but still making an impression. The *New York Times* reported: 'Edward Payson Weston, the father of six-day walking, acted as referee at the finish and made a picturesque appearance encouraging the men as the time grew near the closing hour and running hither and thither up and down the track. He was attired in a long frock coat, glossy tall hat, and was abundantly decorated with ribbons and badges, altogether being the most splendidly dressed man in the Garden.' Later that year, Weston donated a gold and silver belt, the Weston Belt, for another Six-Day Championship of the World.

It was to be several years before he took part in another pedestrian challenge.

In an interview with the *New York Times* in July 1903, he looked back on his career and talked about the hardest part of long walks.

> *If you want to know when I first began to feel like sitting down, it was after I had covered from two to three miles. I tell you candidly that whenever I have started out to walk 100, 200 or even 500 miles, I have felt as though I would give anything and everything I possessed to lie down and rest before I had gone five miles ... Perhaps it is the mental impression of the miles ahead that affects a man. But such a feeling is common among the long-distance walkers, and is very hard to overcome. Once mastered, distance becomes merely a matter of routine.*

The writer then explained that, at the age of 64, Weston still walked 12 to 15 miles a day going about his business in New York, walking to Columbia University where he said he lectured young athletes on how to look after their feet. (In 1907 he said that for the last five years he had earned $200 a week lecturing for 20 weeks of the year.)

Weston told the *Times* that he felt pedestrianism was undergoing a revival but, he said, not the old 'hippodroming' kind of pedestrianism, 'contests filled with so many disagreeable features that the public was disgusted'. He believed that 'pedestrianism is no longer a sport, but a healthful pleasure', like golf, tennis and boating, 'an important factor in outdoor life'.

Three years later, in May 1906, Weston finally got back on the road. For an experiment organised by some of his old doctor friends, he was to walk from Philadelphia to New York in 24 hours, the idea being that the doctors could compare his performance now at the age of 68 with a walk he had done in 1863. The night before the walk started he told reporters: 'I undertake this walk at my age merely to illustrate the advantages of sobriety not only in the performance of feats of endurance but in prolonging physical health strength as well as life.'

During the whole 95-mile trip, Weston took one break and slept for just 25 minutes. The only time he struggled was during a long uphill stretch in the hot May sunshine outside Princeton. He told a reporter for the *Buffalo Illustrated Express*:

> *My old hat was full of ice, but I could not feel a particle of coziness. I knew where I was, but staggered so I feared I might well fall into a ditch. One of my doctor escorts, noticing I was groggy, reached forward to grab me while another met me on*

the run. Sinner that I was, I offered a mental prayer and the thought of my poor mother came to me. I am not over religious, nor am I superstitious, but I can't help thinking that my Christian mother enabled me to fight against that fierce sun until I got to the top of that hill, where I caught a breath of welcome air. I managed to trudge on until I reached New Brunswick, where I struck a mattress and literally fell on it, fast asleep in a second.

Seven doctors gathered around and one exclaimed, 'He's gone! We knew he would collapse. Send for an ambulance quick.' Just as this order was being executed, I opened my eyes and roared, 'Some of you fellows had better get out of here or I'll make you look like 50 cents in less than thirty minutes.' I arose refreshed.

Weston arrived at New York City Hall two minutes late, having missed his ferry from Jersey City to Manhattan. The doctors said that his pulse was normal, though his feet were rather swollen. The *New York Mail* acknowledged a slightly grudging respect for the white-haired athlete:

Edward Payson Weston, the veteran walker, has come in for a universal and almost affectionate admiration after his great feat of Wednesday, because — well, because his old age is so different from the old age of so many professional athletes.

Mr. Weston is neither a saloon keeper nor a sot. He did not burst upon the world for a year or so, 'go the pace' while the pride of youth was upon him, and, like some scores of prizefighters, become a 'good old has-been' at thirty-five. He never felt so fine that it hurt, and he had to get rid of his superfluous energy to the tune of a short life and a merry one. It has not been necessary for pitying friends to organize a benefit for what was left of him. Something better can be said for him than the conventional eulogy of the sport: 'Poor fellow, he was liberal with his money while he had it!' For his demonstration that unusual physical gifts are not of the moment and need not be squandered, but may be husbanded to make old age admirable and delightful, Mr. Weston laid all men in his debt.

It is true that Weston had not dissipated his strength, but he never learned to manage money as wisely as he did his health. Just as well he was in such good shape, then, as he headed towards his seventies, because by 1907 he was broke again and back on the road.

CHAPTER 16

THE

SAW HIM

BEFORE CLUB

BY 1907 WESTON'S NEED TO MAKE SOME MONEY had become pressing. He told a newspaper that he had lost all his savings and property, that they had disappeared 'through no fault of his own'. He did not explain how this had happened — perhaps he had let Maria keep the family home — perhaps he had lost money in some kind of speculation. Anyway, encouraged by his successful Philadelphia to New York hike the year before, he told the paper that another walk was his only option, 'his last resource for raising money'.

His plan was to repeat one of the long trips he had tackled in his twenties; a long journey would give him more opportunities to sell pamphlets and photographs and give lectures along the way. In 1867, at the age of 28, Weston had walked 1,226 miles from Portland, Maine, to Chicago in 26 days (that is, 30 days minus four Sundays). He had marched into Chicago on Thanksgiving, 28th November, to find well-wishers jamming the streets, leaning from every window and lodged in trees and lampposts. Forty years on he hoped to match or even beat that young man's record, and to find the same warm reception.

Ever since the 1870s, when he claimed to be walking for the benefit of science, Weston liked to be able to give an altruistic reason for what he was doing, and he tended to play down his need to raise funds. This time, he said that he hoped to 'revive all over the country interest in pedestrianism' and he wanted to prove that by living a temperate life and taking regular exercise older people could be as fit and strong as the young. Nearly three years before, in January 1905, a very famous doctor, 55-year-old William Osler, had ruffled middle-aged feathers with a speech in which he remarked that men over 40 were useless but those in their 60s were worse: 'the history of the world shows that a very large proportion of the evils may be traced to the sexagenarians – nearly all the great mistakes, politically and socially, all of the worst poems, most of the bad pictures, a majority of the bad novels, not a few of the bad sermons and speeches'. He suggested, jokingly, that men should be chloroformed, 'peacefully extinguished', at 61 (women were a different case as older ones were a good influence on the young). The newspapers, many owned or edited by men of a certain age, leaped on Osler's speech and his comments were still making headlines more than a year later. Weston told the papers that this walk would prove Osler wrong, that he would show that anything the young could do, the old could do better, provided they lived well. Lots of walking, of course, was essential: 'there is no trouble you can't cure with walking', he said. But plenty of prunes and the odd fine cigar were also in order.

Weston left Portland at 5 p.m., on the same date as before, Tuesday 29 October. That morning he told reporters that he had never felt better but admitted to some nerves: 'For weeks my nights have been restless, but Sunday night, I slept like a top. I am anxious to get away.'

As Weston set off, noisy crowds lined the streets as they had in 1867. He was followed by his manager Stanley Rumsley and a doctor travelling by coach, and by a car, a Peerless, full of New York journalists. This was the first time Weston had been accompanied by an automobile and he found that it offered some excellent practical advantages. For one thing, the headlights 'illuminated the road so that it was almost as easy as walking in the daylight'. When the Peerless broke down halfway through the trip, two of Weston's friends turned up in a brand-new $3,000 Gearless Greyhound to light his way to Chicago. These two also turned their car into a rolling buffet for Weston by fixing tin pails full of tea, coffee and milk into the engine to keep warm. The car's speedometer and milometer came in handy too, keeping Weston informed of his 'gait' and how far he had gone.

A few days after the end of the trip, Weston took his first ever ride in a car and said it was 'like sailing on the ocean'. His walk, too, was 1,200 miles of almost plain sailing. The previous time, Weston's progress west from Portland had been dogged by controversy, the newspapers full of accusations that the thing was rigged, that he was in league with bare-knuckle boxers and bent politicians. He had finished his last miles under police protection and in fear of his life. Now, the newspapers were full of respect for the veteran athlete. Weston told one reporter: 'It seemed as though the newspapermen went constantly out of their way to say something kind.' Added to which, the *New York Times* had given him his own column so he was able to make sure his side of the story was heard this time. The only danger he faced was from the overenthusiastic crowds who greeted him all the long way to Chicago.

In Cleveland, Ohio, where 10,000 people heard him speak, unfortunately someone stepped on his heel and rather upset him. In every state,
marching bands, fireworks, cannons and bells greeted the man with the
broad-brimmed hat and white moustache, as they had the youngster in
his regimental uniform, and at every town and village along the route
there were men and women who remembered the young Weston. The
newspapers soon came up with a name, the 'saw-him-before' club, for
all those who were eager to share their reminiscences of the last time
Weston walked by their door.

The country that Weston walked through had changed profoundly
since he had last taken a long American journey. In 1867, America was
only just emerging from the Civil War, the Union had only just been
saved and the reconstruction in the South and the opening up of the
West were its major concerns. Forty years later the USA was becoming
more interested in the world beyond its shores, especially as it looked
for foreign markets for surplus American produce. And, of course,
America looked different too: cinemas and cars were taking the place
of 'travelling panoramas' and horse-drawn coaches, skirts were finally,
slowly, getting shorter and a nation of farmers was on its way to
becoming a land of city dwellers.

But Weston's mind was not on the state of the nation. He later
told a journalist that when he was walking he never looked at the countryside, only at the path in front of his feet. His interests were the state
of the roads, his accommodation and food. The handover of the roads
from horse power to engine power was under way but there had not
yet been any attempt to improve the surfaces; Weston complained that
they were worse than before. In the country, they were still made of

gravel and dirt and, just like in the 1860s, Weston often found himself slithering through ankle-deep mud, or twisting his ankle on frozen ruts. And, of course, the weather was no kinder; Weston struggled on through hail, high winds, snow and freezing rain.

One of the 'saw-him-before' club said Weston's appearance was so much changed he didn't recognise the white-haired walker, but some things would never change. According to one newspaper, Weston still 'cut an attractive figure', and he still cared enough about how he looked to change his clothes before arriving in town. Within a few days of setting off, Weston showed that he was not too old to catch the eye of a pretty girl either as an 18-year-old called Marion Fogg — a 'beautiful vision', said Weston — chased after him on horseback to pin a posy onto his shirt, then cantered ahead to get coffee, eggs and rolls for him. In Plainville, Connecticut, six days into his journey, Weston bowed and raised his hat to the factory girls who 'squealed and shrieked at the old man'.

He had his usual brushes with celebrity too. Whereas in 1867 he had dined with a former and a future president, Millard Fillmore and Grover Cleveland, this time, in Farmington, Connecticut, he was offered tea and eggs by Mrs Anna Roosevelt Cowles, President Theodore's older sister, as he passed her door.

Weston was as emotional as ever, and as the days passed and he was cheered and clapped on his way towards Illinois, he fell in love with America. Writing his *New York Times* column in Erie, Pennsylvania, on 15 November, he effused: 'After a repast I went over to the rink to address an audience ... They were very appreciative and gave me a rousing reception. As I stood in the centre of the rink and looked into that sea of faces that completely surrounded me, I was again made to realise what a glorious country we live in – one that furnished good and noble people.'

This was a very far cry from how he had spoken about America when he returned from England in 1885. Then he had complained that he had always been treated unfairly at home whereas in England he had been treated like a prince. But Weston's feelings always ran with the tide. The *New York Times* described his 'ready emotionalism, and the strain of queerly feminine sentimentality which characterises him'. As long as the crowd loved him, he loved them, and America, back.

The first weeks of Weston's trip ran so smoothly that he was soon ahead of schedule, which meant that a couple of hiccups gave him no concern. In Cleveland he had been refused police protection, was jostled by the crowd and his foot was hurt. In Norwalk, Ohio, he ate too much clam chowder and had to spend a day in bed. But after that, Weston had a clear run and reached his last stop outside Chicago in La Porte, Indiana, on Tuesday 26 November, putting him on course to beat his own time of four decades earlier by 24 hours.

Indiana police accompanied Weston from La Porte as far as the state line, where they handed him over at one in the morning to the Illinois bluecoats. Hundreds of people carrying torches were waiting to greet him, along with 'lines of automobiles stretch[ed] out behind like a caravan' and they kept him company all the way to his hotel on the lake front, seven miles from the city centre.

He arrived at the Chicago Beach Hotel at three in the morning and sat up, tired and dusty, to write his piece for the front page of the *New York Times*. He had had his best day's walking covering a little more than 95 miles since leaving Ligonier, Indiana, a few minutes after midnight on Tuesday, and his most 'enthusiastic' day too. In South Bend, Indiana, he spoke to the townspeople from a hotel balcony and found another 'considerate' and 'applauding' crowd in his next stop, La Porte.

Weston slept for a few hours then got dressed for his last day on the road. In a blue plaid suit, black gaiters, black felt hat and white gloves, and the same shoes he had worn to win the Astley Belt 28 years earlier, Weston left his room at 9.45 a.m. He paused for a moment in the hotel lobby, gazing at the crowd and tugging at his white moustache, before swooping through the doors to launch into his last lap.

The committee and judges followed him by car and a line of 12 policemen walked ahead of him. A double file of men walked either side of him holding ropes which were tied to the car behind Weston, making a mobile enclosure to keep the crowd to the side. He reached the post office on Jackson Boulevard at 12.10 p.m., breaking his old time by 26 hours and 25 minutes. Alderman Badernoch witnessed Weston's arrival in good time and then an awkward moment followed as an official refused to let Weston in the main entrance, where he was supposed to be greeted by Mayor Fred Busse.

Weston turned on his heel and walked away, asking directions to the Illinois Athletic Club on Michigan Avenue, where he was due for lunch a little later. The crowd followed him and thousands waited in the street outside the club. Weston gave a speech on a balcony above the entrance:

> *I have stayed on my feet right along during this walk, but if*
> *anything could take me off my foot it would be the greeting you*

have given me today. I want to tell you that it is appreciated.

I want to tell you another thing, and that is this — that this walk proves that an American, however old he may be, can beat the world at walking.

I am feeling fine, and after I've rested up for a week or so I'll be ready to go and do the whole walk over again. I want to tell you that I feel as fit as I ever did in my life and by next week I'll be ready to walk anybody of whatever age as long as he likes.

I have met nothing but kindness along this trip. Everywhere I've gone I've met the same hearty American greeting and the same hearty American kindness. If any of you do not fully realize what a great country you are living in you should take a pedestrian trip like the one I've just finished.

It is a great delight to me to be back in Chicago and to realize that I can walk all the way from Portland ... to your city in better time than I did it forty years ago, when I was a young man.

'This is the most enjoyable occasion of my life,' he concluded. 'I walked to Chicago for glory. I wanted to do my part to show all Englishmen, Frenchmen, Germans, Australians, and other nations that Americans can beat them at everything on the cards.'

He then retired to change into black frock coat, striped trousers, wing collar and red tie in time for lunch. After lunch he posed for photographers in the club gymnasium, showing off the feet that had walked so many thousands of miles. In the evening he lounged around the club, watched some games in the swimming pool and went to bed saying he 'hardly felt he had done a day's work'.

After two days of being dined and feted in the city, he jokingly complained that his 'iron constitution' was near to collapse, broken by a surfeit of turkey, cranberries and mince pies. But in truth, Weston was head over heels, overflowing with love and gratitude for how his walk had been received. America was the best nation in the world and, he told journalists, Chicago had the most beautiful women in America: 'This lake breeze gives them a healthy glow to their cheeks, makes their eyes bright, and keeps their skin clear.'

But, if he had love, he still had no money. Weston reckoned the trip had cost him $1 per mile in expenses, and that sales of pamphlets and tickets for his lectures had only just covered the cost. He alleged that one of his agents, Dana Patten, had not handed over proceeds from lectures and appearances along the route.

The next year he was still seeking an income, giving lectures and exhibitions. In May 1908 his search for a living took him as far as California, where he walked from San Francisco to Los Angeles, 512 miles in 12 days, at the age of 69.

CHAPTER

OCEAN TO OCEAN

WESTON HAD FIRST TALKED ABOUT WALKING ACROSS AMERICA in 1869 when he was 30 years old. The newspapers had jeered at the suggestion and said the Apaches would get him, but it was an irresistible challenge. The big, wild space opening out to the west was a mountain he had to climb, an adventure he could not say no to, rather like his father's bout of gold fever. Really, he was no different from thousands of other Americans who had gone west before him, except that he only wanted to walk the country, not mine or farm it.

He next mentioned the idea in 1884 when he was nearly 45, shortly after his 5,000-mile walk around England, when he promised Sir John Astley that he would go west on his 70th birthday. In January 1909 he began to make firm plans to do what he had dreamed of for so many years. By then, Sir John was gone (he had died in 1894) and so were the Apaches. Weston would begin his transcontinental hike, as promised, on his 70th birthday, Monday 15 March 1909.

He chose a vintage year for travel, coming at the end of a decade that was finding new and faster ways of getting about. In 1909, Louis

Bleriot crossed the Channel by plane and an English aviator, Henri Farman, made the first 100-mile flight. Two men, H. Nelson Jackson and Sewall K. Crocker, and a bulldog named Bud made the first motor trip across the continent in 1903, driving from San Francisco to New York in 63 days. By the time Weston set off, the record time for a car journey from San Francisco to New York was 15 days 2 hours and 10 minutes, done in a Franklin car in August 1906; from New York to San Francisco the record was 24 days, 8 hours and 45 minutes. A train, the Harriman Special, had done the trip in 71 hours and 27 minutes, and the record time for a motor bike was 30 days and 12 hours. Even while Weston was walking, Alice Ramsey became the first woman to drive across America.

All the more reason for Weston to take up the challenge. Another one came in the form of marathon running, which gained sudden popularity in America when a US athlete, Johnny Hayes, won gold in the marathon at the 1908 Olympics in London. Pedestrianism had been in decline since its peak of popularity in the 1870s and '80s and Weston worried that the new craze for running would finish it for good. He hoped that his hike to San Francisco would become a challenge to young athletes, telling reporters: 'Well, I'll be off for another good-sized walk pretty soon. I'm going clear across the continent this time and hope to set a mark that even the youngsters won't touch for a while.'

The 4,300-mile distance from New York to San Francisco was shorter than his English temperance jaunt, again to be done in 100 days, but, of course, it would be a completely different experience. In little England, Weston had had to follow a meandering, winding route and do more miles in halls and rinks to make up the distance. Wherever his walk took him, he was never far from a town or city.

On his American route, towns and villages would become few and far between as he reached the West and only a few hundred miles of road were paved, the rest were clay, sand and loose stones; although cars were selling in greater numbers each year, there had still been no improvement to the roads. The *Auburn Citizen* described the task Weston had set himself: 'Four miles an hour for 10 consecutive hours daily, Sunday excepted, through sand and clay, rain and shine, o'er mountains and across the plains ... Only to persons who have walked with Weston is the significance of his task appreciated. It is next to impossible to grasp the fullness until you have plowed through mud and slush, up hill and down with this indomitable little man.'

The *New York Times* consulted a panel of doctors about the likelihood of Weston managing such a gruelling feat. Dr Frederic Brush of the New York Post-Graduate Medical School scotched Weston's claim, which he frequently insisted on, that what he was doing anyone his age could do if they stayed fit. 'I look on Weston personally as a most remarkable man; a man of extraordinary individual equipment. It is absurd to say that he shows only what men who, starting with good physiques, could do at his age with careful training. They can't. Why, he is doing what mighty few young men, young athletes can do. No man of any age at all had ever come up to his record so far as I know.'

Dr George L. Meyland of Columbia University said:

> *I wouldn't prophesy as to whether he can finish. If it were not for*
> *his walk last year from Portland to Chicago, I wouldn't think it*
> *possible, but that makes a man ready to believe anything of him.*

He has the mechanism of walking to perfection — the ability to use just the minimum of energy in covering a given space. Of course, he has the 'bent-knee' method ... the body forward, and the leg muscles used only in the middle of their range. It's just the natural way to walk; our stiff-legged method, product of high hats, stiff clothes, and canes is purely artificial.

In early March, Weston announced his planned route. It was several hundred miles longer than it needed to be because he had decided to avoid Cleveland where in 1907 he had been refused police protection and was jostled and hurt by the crowd; Weston never forgot an insult or injury. From New York he was to walk west as far as Buffalo, then turn southward to Pittsburgh and north again to Chicago, giving Cleveland a very wide berth. From Chicago, where the Illinois Athletic Club was planning a reception for him, his route would take him south again to St Louis, then west through Kansas and Denver, all the way through Salt Lake and Nevada to San Francisco. As far as possible, he planned to follow the same route as the railroads, which was shorter than the post-road route. He would be accompanied by another new manager, Charles Hagan, and an attendant, Ward Cassells, travelling by car. Journalists from various cities would drive parts of the route with him too.

On the morning of his birthday, a few hours before departing, Weston posed for a photographer for the *Sporting News*. He stretched and strutted, bending forward and holding his cane behind his back to show how he liked to walk uphill. He wanted the pictures to show that his body was stronger and more limber than his white moustache and balding head might suggest: 'But here! Take me from the side. I want to show you there is no bend in my back that they say old men always get. Now, I'm ready, just as if I were going to take a step. Shoot!'

He told journalists: 'I'll feel that my life work has been completed if I can prove to the young men of the country that God made them to walk, and that if they walk they'll be healthy.'

While this went on, thousands of people gathered outside the New York General Post Office building to witness Weston's departure. Expected in the postmaster Edward Morgan's office at 4.15 p.m., Edward was a few minutes late. Suddenly, said the *New York Times,* 'the swinging doors were thrown wide open, and Weston raced into the middle of the floor, attired in a long, linen duster'. He shook a few hands, then headed down the steps of the building to the street, shrugging off his long coat as he went. In a blue lightweight coat, riding trousers, 'natty mouse-colored leggings and a felt hat of broad brim that resembled a sombrero in all but color', Weston was sent on his way, on time, at 4.30 p.m., to start the first of 4,300 miles.

Mounted police, members of his old regiment, the seventh New York State National Guard and a marching band kept pace with him and held the dense crowd at bay as Weston marched up Lafayette Avenue. At 59th Street the band struck up 'Auld Lang Syne', as the soldiers peeled off and left the walking to Weston. The *New York Times* wrote: 'Walking with elasticity of step and freedom of action that was the absolute contradiction of age, Edward Payson Weston, the veteran pedestrian, celebrated the seventy-first anniversary [actually the seventieth] of his birth yesterday afternoon by starting one of the longest walks of his career.'

Weston had again been signed up by the *Times* to write exclusive updates for its readers. On his first night, in Tarrytown where he arrived after midnight, he wrote: 'I arrived here at 12.30 this morning, feeling in the best of health and spirits. The reception that was extended to me in New York, at Yonkers, and along the route was the greatest I have ever witnessed, and I am indeed truly grateful to those who appreciated the start of my effort.'

LEAVING NEW YORK IN MARCH, Weston walked straight into the tail-end of the fierce New England winter. The roads and weather in New York State knocked him off schedule within days. Snow fell in the hills and the muddy roads were frozen into ruts, forcing Weston to weave from one side to the other to avoid the worst of the troughs and ridges. As he went on his way across the continent, forging through hundreds of miles each week, the weather would be his faithful enemy. He waded through floods in Illinois and was astounded by the climate in the Midwest, the speed and force of the storms that chased and harried him across the prairies. In July, in the Nevada desert, he cooked.

However, the frigid Eastern weather did not spoil the warmth with which Weston's fans greeted him. His arrival in Syracuse on 22 March was reported in the *Times*: 'Down the easy grade leading toward the centre of the city marched the old man, who is seventy-one years young, silvery head up like a grenadier's, white moustache militant, his hat swinging easily in his hand. Right and left he bowed to the throng that had gathered swift as a storm upon the walks, and as he marched his attendant bodyguard grew and grew until the utmost effort was required by those in charge to clear the way.'

In a restaurant on West Fayette Street, Weston asked the waiter for paper so he could get started on his column for the *Times*. He wrote that that day he had been 'hauling [his] hoofs out of mud like mucilage', but that more and more people recognised him from the newspapers and stopped to greet him on the road, and whatever time of the night he might trundle into a town or village, people would come out of their houses to cheer him on his way.

WESTON SOON MADE UP THE TIME he had lost in snowy New York State but hit a new difficulty. The poor roads were tough to walk on (where they were too bad, Weston would step off the road and walk through the fields and orchards) but they were catastrophic for the car carrying his manager, his nurse and his baggage. Outside Cambridge Springs, Pennsylvania, the car got stuck in a mud-hole. By the time it was dug out and restarted, Weston was several days and 138 miles in the lead. He finally met up with his car, and his clothes, again in Bellevue, Ohio, only to lose it for good in Chicago. It seems whoever had sold his friends the car had agreed to take responsibility for repairs and replacement parts, but this had turned out to be more onerous than the sellers had expected and now the car was getting poor publicity too.

From Chicago, Weston made his way to the Chicago and Alton railroad and walked along the tracks. The railway route was harder to walk on but shorter than the country roads. He learned to read the block signals so he would know if a train was coming, though he did get a little spooked while crossing a 150-feet-high bridge, wondering what he would do if a train came. He arrived in Missouri on 28 April and at Mexico, Missouri, on Sunday 2 May began to question for the first time whether he would make his target. He had had a poor week, having been held up by freezing gales and rain. He had also had several falls that week. During the weeks of his walk across the continent, he had many falls, far more than he had suffered in previous walks. He at one point said, 'It is only when I do some foolish thing that I am made to realise that I am a trifle older than I was twenty-five years ago.' For the first time, Weston acknowledged a little frailty. And as he went further into the West, further from home, he appeared frail and vulnerable for the first time too.

By the time he reached Kansas he was travelling alone, except for on the odd stretch where someone, a young student or local bigwig, walked alongside him for a day or two. For the most part, the 70-year-old pedestrian had only his own shadow for company on the wide Midwestern plains. Near Buffalo Park, Kansas, Weston's path crossed the route of that year's Glidden Tour, an annual rally set up by the Automobile Association of America to promote motoring. One of the drivers, a Mr Meinzinger, told a newspaper: 'It was a pathetic sight – or rather so it appeared to us to see the lone old man coming across the prairie.' The motorists stopped to chat with Weston who 'couldn't stand still for a minute, but kept shifting from one foot to the other as he talked'. Still, Weston seemed chipper and, thinking no doubt of the car he had left behind in Chicago, he teased the drivers about his 'superior ability to ford swollen creeks and skip over mud-holes'.

By 19 May Weston was in Sharon Springs, getting ready to hike his last 30 miles in Kansas before crossing into Colorado. He wrote: 'In leaving Kansas, I want to say that though I have traveled all over England and part of France and a large part of America, thus far I have never yet passed through such a beautiful and health-giving country and such genial and hospitable people as are located in the Sunflower State. To me it has been a paradise in every town and village I passed. Someone would invariably appear with some refreshing drink.'

As he got further west, however, he found it increasingly difficult to get either food or accommodation. Weston did not carry food with him and had to rely on ranchers and station agents to help him. His road was a lonely one: 'Colorado is sparsely settled across the Union Pacific Railway. The towns are very small, and accommodations are not of the best. I have walked fifteen miles without meeting a person; an occasional rabbit, many prairie dogs and coyotes the only "live ones" to greet me.'

In Colorado, the weather alternately soaked and blow-dried him. When his manager and luggage were held up by delayed trains, he said it didn't matter, the rain would wash his clothes as he walked. From Nunn, Colorado, he telegraphed the *New York Times*:

> *The people east of Chicago have no idea of the force and magnitude of the elements of the West. Compared with the showers and breezes in the East they are awful and past comprehension. The showers come suddenly and in torrents and you are drenched to the skin. Within the past two weeks I have been wet through a dozen times, and the houses are so far apart*

*I have been forced to walk to dry my clothes. One day in the week
of May 17, I walked thirty-six miles before I could get breakfast
or have a rest, and for twenty-two miles did not see a house.*

His road was about to get lonelier. In June, Weston crossed
the state border into Wyoming, where he found the country raw and
desolate. From Rock River, he wrote: 'I had all sorts of experiences
yesterday. I passed through a tunnel half a mile long which gave me the
horrors. Snow is everywhere in evidence from recent storms. The massive hills, full of large rocks and decomposed granite, make such a wild,
lonesome picture.' But on the other hand, the road bed was granite,
'the best I have ever walked upon'.

His only company was the 'section hands', the men working on
each section of the railroad. Settlements were 15 or 20 miles apart and
between them he would find nothing but 'section houses', hostels for
the railroad workers 'filled to capacity with section hands; nationality
Greeks, Italians or Japanese'.

In wild Wyoming, Weston was unnerved by his isolation and by
some of his fellow travellers. Filing his column from Granger, 60 or
so miles from the border with Utah, he complained: 'Another great
annoyance is the hoboes who travel along the railroads stealing rides on
freight trains whenever possible and some of them don't look good to
me. I am now carrying a revolver, but for what purpose I hardly know,
believing that if I were attacked they would also take my gun.'

The weather too continued to trouble him. In Medicine Bow, he
wrote that the conditions he had coped with since leaving Kansas had
been the worst he had ever experienced in 45 years of walking: 'There

is hardly a day in which I don't encounter some extreme elements of weather, such as wind storm and sudden rains, snow, hail, or sleet. However encouraging the indication may be on starting out, invariably I am caught when miles away from any town or haven of safety. I am never sure of reaching the destination for the day.'

The landscape of southern Wyoming, the low, dry bare-backed hills, gave no comfort to a man from green, woodsy New England: 'The country itself affords no encouragement for one engaged in a task of this kind.' A few miles away from Medicine Bow in Hanna, a storm blew the walker off the railroad, 30 feet to the bottom of an embankment. Walking past Hanna Colliery No I, where hundreds of men had died in an explosion in 1903, confirmed his impression of a hostile, hard-living country. Further on , another fall caused him another injury. He was carrying a glass bottle tucked into his belt and it broke when he fell, cutting his belly. At Rawlins, 2,787 miles and 73 days into his route, Weston was again soaked by rain. He had so far averaged a little more than 38 miles per day; to reach San Francisco in 27 more days he would have to do better.

WHEN HE FINALLY MADE IT INTO UTAH, on 18 June, Weston's delight and relief at exiting Wyoming with its storms and hoboes tumbled out of him in exuberant praise of 'Mormonland'. 'By gum, this is God's country, isn't it?' he exclaimed to a local newsman. 'Why, do you know, as I crossed the line from Wyoming the grass began to grow on this side within two inches from the post, by thunder! And it's been getting greener and thicker ever since.' Dressed in knickerbockers, a ruffled shirt, à broad-brimmed straw hat 'crushed to a pancake', in need of a shave and haircut and with his pistol and water bottle tucked into his belt, Weston cut a noticeably rougher figure than the nifty one that marched out of New York, but he said he was confident that he would succeed.

At Ogden, Utah, with 900 miles to go and just 18 days to do it, there came a breakthrough; he would no longer be travelling alone. 'Joy has come at last,' he wrote. The railway company had arranged for one of its employees, Joseph Murray, to follow Weston on a 'gasoline rail velocipede' loaded with refreshments, and every dining car on the line had orders to keep him supplied with ice. Despite that joy, however, Weston's journey was about to reach its toughest stretch yet as his route took him straight across the Nevada desert. Here, he encountered a new foe as the temperature hit 102oF and the mosquitoes found him.

Writing from Battle Mountain, Nevada, on 29 June he reported:

> *I arrived here very late last night and was completely exhausted by my insane endeavor to kill mosquitoes. Fancy one being on a broad, almost uninhabited, prairie, not a tree to be seen, nothing but sage brush and black clouds of mosquitoes, whose activity would shame the New Jersey variety. The heat is so intense that the natives complain. It was 90°F in the shade this morning and about 5°F warmer in the hotels. Rest is out of the question, and while evening is somewhat cooler the insects will drive one frantic.*

The heatwave continued into July and Weston started to walk

during the night, or the early hours of morning and the evening, and tried to sleep in the day. From Lovelock, 3,547 miles from New York, Weston wired to the *Times*: 'Two weeks on the Great American Desert. Is it any wonder I long for something else than sand, alkali, tremendous heat, mosquitoes, and sage brush. There is nothing here that tends to encouragement or induce pleasant walking. One who has never traveled in these parts could not possibly imagine the conditions. Loud complaints are heard from those traveling by rail through this section. What would they say if they walked?'

Weston was exhausted by the heat and fell days behind his schedule. From Lovelock, he had just five days walking time left and the High Sierra standing between him and the Pacific. An engineer from the Southern Pacific Railway met him in Reno to guide him through 42 miles of snow sheds but, even with that help, by 10 July, a day after he had been due to finish his journey, Weston was in Auburn, California, where his father had searched for gold 60 years before, still some 120 miles from San Francisco.

Weston was flattened by what seemed to him like failure. In Roseville, the next day, he wrote: 'If any one had told me six months ago that I would undertake to walk over railroad tracks between Chicago and San Francisco for 2,577 miles, and practically without attendance or necessary refreshments for 1,800 miles of that distance, I would have said, "I am not such an idiot." I am not saying this to excuse this wretched failure. I am simply stating facts ... This is the most crushing failure I have encountered in my career.'

Weston finally arrived in San Francisco at 11 o'clock at night on 14 July, five days too late. In his last despatch to the *Times*, he wrote:

Regarding my feelings and condition, I would say that I feel like uttering bitter words, but do not feel inclined to make excuses.

I have received hundreds of letters and telegrams congratulating me on my wonderful achievement, and each one makes me wish I deserved it. Full of vigor and strength, I am disappointed that the elements were against me, and I frankly acknowledge that had it not been for the unbounded kindness of the officers and employees of the Southern Pacific Railroad Company, I should not have dared to come further than Ogden, Utah. I practically had the right of way on the railroad, and every engineer tooted the whistle on the engine as it passed me.

But Weston believed that he had racked up hundreds of extra miles in crossing back and forth from one side of the road and the railway to the other to find the best footing:

I contend I walked a distance of upward of 4,000 miles in 104 days and 5 hours, and while it exceeds the distance between New York and San Francisco [by] nearly 700 miles, and far excels any previous record, yet technically it is a failure, and I do not feel inclined to close my public career with a failure.

The expenses of this walk were upward of $2,500. Some dozen prominent cities in the East have made offers to arrange for testimonial lectures on my return not only to help liquidate my financial loss but to show that my object lesson in the journey, in striving to elevate in popular esteem the exercise of walking, is appreciated.

He began immediately to plan a repeat attempt in order to vindicate himself, to erase his failure, even if other people thought he had achieved something amazing:

> *If within the next two weeks I shall receive assurances from a sufficient number of cities and towns between Omaha and New York that they will arrange for lectures and send such word to me in care of the Southern Pacific Railroad Company, San Francisco, then I will try to prove myself worthy of their confidence and esteem by showing how easy it be for any one to walk from San Francisco to New York by direct route within 100 secular days.*
>
> *There are three very dear friends who energetically oppose this extra walk, but when I convince them that it is my only salvation, and that it would still keep me young and healthy, I know they will fall in with my plans. Meanwhile, the only trouble I have is an awful appetite.*

The rematch, Weston versus the American continent part two, took place the following year. The 'grand old man of the open road' left New York on a train for Los Angeles on 24 January 1910, the week after the first International Aviation Meet took place in the city. An Illinois newspaper described Weston as an evangelist for walking, protesting against modern transport which was making Americans lazy: 'That Weston at seventy-two is going to walk across the American continent in 100 days is really an epochal piece of news. Airships are "in the air". Automobiles are everywhere. Urban and interurban trolleys are taking the place of Shank's mare.' Weston was not, apparently, walking on a wager, he was 'too big an institution for that'; he was walking to save America's youth from idleness.

Weston left Santa Monica on 1 February at 4 p.m., aiming to arrive in New York 106 days later on 17 May – which left only 90 days available for walking. This time he made astounding progress and leaped ahead of his schedule within weeks.

Reporting of the early part of Weston's second transcontinental hike was patchy. The *New York Times* had not renewed his contract so there were no columns this time, but his progress was recorded in local newspapers along the way and one or two letters which Weston wrote to friends in New York were published. In one of these, written in Albuquerque on 28 February, he told his friend that the same winds that had battered him and slowed him down on his way to San Francisco in 1909 were now blowing him swiftly eastwards towards New York, helping him walk faster. In the same letter, he set out exactly what he aimed to achieve with this new walk:

> *In this across-the-continent effort I propose to make three records: First to show that if it had not been my mistake to go from New York to San Francisco instead of from San Francisco to New York I could easily have made the 4,000 miles in 100 days; second, to make a record from Santa Monica, 18 miles west of Los Angeles, to New York (from ocean to ocean), walking 3,500 miles, that no one not under 65 years of age will be able to equal during the present century.*
>
> *The third is perhaps the most important of all. I will make a record between Chicago and New York (1,054 miles) that it*

will make a man of any age hustle to excel, and to show that the
2,500 miles previously walked are, instead of a detriment, of
valuable assistance.

In New Mexico, he told reporters that he believed he would reach New York a week early and win himself a prize of $3,500: $500 for each day he knocked off his 90-day schedule.

Crossing from New Mexico into Colorado on Monday 7 March, Weston arrived in the town of Trinidad to find that the public schools had been shut so the children would have the chance to see Weston whirling through their town. A few days later, Weston was in Kansas, more than 1,600 miles into his hike, celebrating his birthday by walking 72 miles from Ingalls to Garfield. The *New York Globe* revealed exactly what the birthday boy had eaten and drunk over the 72 miles: 14 eggs, four bowls of oatmeal, a dish of prunes, five slices of bread, 12 griddle cakes, two bowls of hot chocolate, a half-pound of chocolate, three cups of coffee, five pints of milk and a pot of tea.

The next day Weston slept in until 11 a.m., then set off for his next stop, 36 miles away. A few miles outside town he was nearly hit by a car but suffered nothing more serious than a little bruising. A doctor checked him over and declared that he was fine and had the physique of a 35-year-old.

A week later Weston's private life was in the news as an Illinois paper revealed that Mrs Weston was also in Kansas. The *Decatur Review* had tracked down Maria in Kansas City, where she was visiting their younger daughter Maud but had avoided her estranged husband when he passed through the town. Maria had been there for a few months, on holiday from her home in Brooklyn. The paper said: 'She is about 65 years old, rather plump and of motherly, kind appearance. And she's pleasant too, except when one thing is mentioned — her husband and the separation. "I just don't care to discuss it," she said to a visitor this morning.'

By the end of March, arriving in Missouri ten days ahead of time, Weston was starting to show signs of trouble. He was struggling to cope with the hot weather and a number of falls had left him with cuts and bruises all over his shins and knees. Some newspapers began to question whether he would even make it to Chicago, let alone New York, but the *New York Times* was more concerned about how Weston had managed to get so far ahead of his own timetable:

> *It is believed that Weston made many mistakes in figuring the different distances he was to walk each day, and this is the reason why he is so far ahead of his schedule time. As the reports kept coming in day after day, showing that the old pedestrian was hiking along far in excess of the speed he had planned on traveling, it may give the impression that the veteran walker was accomplishing an almost impossible performance. Weston is accomplishing a great feat in tramping across the continent, but his daily tramps are not in actual distance what his schedule shows them to be.*

Weston was not giving any lectures during this trip so his only income would be the $500 he was to win for each day he shaved from his schedule. Quite possibly, he had written himself an itinerary which would guarantee him a decent pay-out when he reached New York.

Anyway, apart from the *Times,* no one seemed to care whether Weston had fiddled the numbers or not; there was no arguing with the fact that this wiry, white-haired 72-year-old had walked thousands of miles all the way from the Pacific Ocean. He quickly recovered from the aches and pains that troubled him in Missouri, reached Chicago on Monday 4 April and soon arrived in New England where friends and celebrities waited to congratulate him.

Arriving in Buffalo, New York State, on 18 April, Weston was 16 days ahead. Here he was introduced to Alfie Shrubb, a world-record-breaking English runner. Weston recommended that Shrubb quit running and take up pedestrianism: 'I'm glad to meet you,' he told him, 'but I must say that the inventor of the marathon should be electrocuted. The process works the human machine under a killing pressure and must result in general breakdown in the end. It is not to be compared with walking, but, of course I congratulate you on your success in this particular field of athletics. Take up walking my boy and live to reach a ripe old age.' (Shrub ignored his advice and died in 1964 aged 84.)

In Chittenango Weston received a bagful of post, including a letter from Macklyn Arbuckle, brother of the more famous Fatty, telling him he was a wonderful example to young and old the world over. Another letter, from some of his friends and sponsors, was a copy of a circular that they had sent out to raise a subscription for him. Outside Syracuse, Weston was joined by the actors Thomas A. Wise and Douglas Fairbanks, who were appearing in the play 'A Gentleman from Mississippi' at the city's Wieting theatre.

There had been more car trouble for Weston, and more was to come. At Palmyra, Pennsylvania, the car that was accompanying him blundered into a ditch and took his provisions with it. He had already lost one car, wrecked in a crash with a handcar in California. Furthermore, following his near miss in New Mexico, Weston was increasingly unnerved and exasperated by sharing the road with cars. In a couple of places drivers had hurried up behind him then sounded their horn, making him jump with fright. At the end of April, near Albany, Weston was walking with a 20-year-old man, Guy Lewis, when the youngster was brushed by a passing car. Lewis fell onto Weston and nearly knocked him out. The *New York Times* writer who reported the incident wrote that he 'picked the old man up in his arms, and found he was so dazed he could not stand alone'. But Weston refused further help. He sat down on the grass at the side of the road, shocked and with a painful, swollen ankle. He was taken to rest in a farmhouse nearby and was well enough next morning to continue, limping, towards New York.

This was not the last time Weston would be hurt by a car, but the next few days, as he drew nearer and nearer to New York City, were uneventful. Arriving in Yonkers, his last stop before New York, Weston was joined by Annie, described here as his niece. Annie told the papers, 'I was surprised at father's splendid condition, I expected to find him much thinner and a trifle wan, but instead he is lively, in good flesh and the color of a cherry. I am proud of him, and I hope the American people will understand why he made this wonderful journey as an example to the youth of America.'

Weston told reporters: 'It was a great walk, all right, and I'm glad it has ended as happily as it has. It's good to be back, and I guess I've taken my last walk. It's up to the young men now. The public doesn't care anything about me, except as a sort of curiosity, a young old man.

That's all there is to it.'

The next day, 2 May, Weston walked into New York City 13 days early, with his bad ankle still wrapped in bandages. By the time he reached Manhattan there were already thousands of people on the streets. As he made his way down Broadway, a growing mass of people followed him. At the Ansonia Hotel on 73rd Street he stopped for apple pie and tea, leaving his crowd of companions waiting outside.

A little further on, at the southeast corner of Central Park, 10,000 people were packed into Columbus Circle; in Time Square 15,000 were waiting for him, waving handkerchiefs and throwing flowers. According to one estimate, a total of 500,000 people turned out to fill Broadway that day, to watch Weston, the 'young old man', on his last miles. One newspaper said that he 'was the object of an ovation such as has rarely been accorded to any individual short of a victorious admiral or a colonel of the rough riders regiment'.

Forging through the crowd, he made his way to the City Hall, 'white locks bared to the breeze and his shuffling feet keeping time to the "Star Spangled Banner"'. At 3.10 p.m. in front of 25,000 onlookers he climbed the building's steps.

He was met by William Jay Gaynor, the Mayor of New York City. Without saying a word, Weston handed over a letter from Mayor George Alexander of Los Angeles. Gaynor read the letter, then, as tears rolled down Weston's sunburned cheeks, the mayor paid tribute to the walker's achievement:

> *I thank you for bringing to me in such an extraordinary manner*
> *this letter from Mayor George Alexander of Los Angeles. People*

ought to do like you and live as much as possible in the open air. If they did, they'd live to be 100 years old right here.

My old friend, I am mighty proud of you and the whole world ought to be proud of you. You started on February the 1st at four o'clock and got here on May the 2nd at 3:10 o'clock. This is marvellous, simply marvellous.

There was never anything like it in the history of the world ... By your success in crossing the continent in 78 days you have surpassed every feat of ancient or modern times.

Later in the day, as he recovered, Weston predicted that he would do no more long walks, just the usual '10 or 12 miles every day to keep in condition'. He planned to spend the rest of his seventies lecturing. In August 1910, the Edward Payson Long Wear Hose for Men was launched, costing 25 cents per pair.

His prediction was wrong though. In 1913, at the age of 74, Weston walked 1,500 miles from New York to Minneapolis in 60 days. An old rival, John Ennis, now 71, tried to overtake and beat him but became unwell, and Weston reached Minneapolis in time on 2 August 1913, where he laid the mortar for the cornerstone of a new clubhouse for the Minneapolis Athletics Club.

In 1914, Weston moved out of the Bronx to the countryside. He bought a farm in upstate New York and took Annie there to live with him. He had decided, at the age of 75, that it was time to live a quieter life.

CHAPTER 18

THE END

OF EVERYTHING

WESTON REACHED HIS EIGHTIES STILL IN GOOD HEALTH and still walking in 1919, the year prohibition was written into the American constitution and a year before women (middle-class women, anyway) got the vote. Since his walk from the Pacific to the Atlantic and his rapturous reception in New York, everything had changed. America had entered the Great War in 1917, and sent a million soldiers to Europe. At the same time as it launched itself unhappily into the affairs of the outside world, America closed its doors to the world with new laws that put an end to the great waves of immigration that had been a defining feature of America's 19th century.

With the end of the war came the Jazz Age, Gatsby's decade of champagne, speakeasies, skyscrapers and daring knee-length skirts. But fun and prosperity were for the few: although wages increased and unemployment fell, nearly half of all families lived on less than $1,000 per year, while businessmen and architects were building their Manhattan castles in the air, millions of New Yorkers still lived in condemned tenements. Poverty was not restricted to the big cities either. The cotton and textile industries were in trouble and farmers were being driven off the land because an overabundance of food had wrecked the prices they could get for their produce.

Weston was living quietly in the countryside in upstate New York, trying to pay off his debts as he had tried so many times before. In 1921 a Wisconsin paper, the Appleton Post–Crescent, reported that the 82-year-old planned, fancifully, to recreate his record-breaking walk of December 1874 when he made 500 miles in six days for the first time at the Newark Rink. In the meantime, he was lecturing, trying to earn money: 'He wants to collect enough money to finish payment of a $10,000 debt contracted on his last cross-country hike, declaring he wishes to face his Maker with a clean slate.'

The following year he did tackle a 500-mile walk, a rather less intense one from Buffalo to New York in 30 days rather than six. In a khaki suit, open-necked shirt and white bandsman's cap, he set off from Buffalo on Tuesday 5 September 1922 accompanied by his manager Walter Spencer and Annie O'Hagan in a horse and buggy. The *Utica Herald Dispatch* wrote that he cut a 'picturesque' figure: 'His hair is snow white and a long white moustache adds that touch that completes the picture of a typical New England Yankee.' According to the *Poughkeepsie Eagle-News*, the 83-year-old was still 'possessed of sound mind and a remarkable sense of humor. Indeed, he mentioned a "sense of humor" as a prime essential to endurance. "When you are all in, or think you are," said Mr Weston, "think of something funny and you will forget your tiredness."'

Even if his gait was a little 'tottering' these days, Weston made good progress and the distance gave him no trouble. His only complaint was that cars were crowding him off the road. By the 1920s there were millions of motor vehicles on America's roads and each year thousands of pedestrians died in traffic accidents. Weston told the *Syracuse Herald* that he intended to stop off in Albany, the state capital, and urge the governor to compel drivers to sound their horn when overtaking pedestrians. But despite his concerns, Edward made it safely to New York. He arrived two days ahead of schedule on Thursday 5 October, in time to find the City Hall surrounded by baseball fans who had gathered round the bulletin boards showing results from the World Series game taking place uptown.

NEARLY TWO YEARS AFTER THAT WALK, Weston made news across the United States with a very different story. On 16 May 1924, the *New York Times* carried the headline: 'E.P. Weston, 86, is Shot in Attack on Home'. On his farm in 'the wilds of the Plutarch Mountains' in Ulster County, New York State, a gang of men had reportedly attacked the 85-year-old (the newspapers again having added a year to his age).

The story continued:

> Armed with sticks and rocks and at least one gun, the gang stormed the house. The old man made what resistance he could unarmed and finally barricaded himself in one room in the upper part of the house. The gang continued to throw large rocks and clubs at the windows until not a pane of glass or a window sash remained in the house. They finally forced their way into the room upstairs, in which Weston made a desperate stand for a

man of his years. But he was cornered and severely beaten, and
during the attack was shot in the leg.

The *Times* commented that Weston had made his home in Highland, a tiny hamlet in a wild, wooded part of Ulster County inhabited by 'many people of questionable character' who had no obvious means of supporting themselves and who made a living selling wood cut from other people's land. Several abandoned farms had recently been bought up by incomers and some of these 'lawless residents' resented the new arrivals. Or, said the *Times,* it could have been a drunken spree. The paper added that 'for some time law-abiding residents in this section have been terrified by this lawless element, and many residents have been forced to arm themselves'.

There was, however, another theory. Under the headline 'Weston Shooting Laid to Woman Living in House', the *Oakland Tribune* of California reported that the police had a theory 'that Weston was attacked by mountaineers [locals] who were incensed by the presence of the unmarried woman in his home'. The paper described Annie as Weston's sister's daughter who he had adopted as his own.

Annie told a journalist that any suggestion that it was her relationship with Weston that had inspired the attack was 'ridiculous', and she kept up the pretence that she was his daughter: 'Daddy is a poor man for whom I care a great deal. I will always take care of him. I want him to live as long as possible and that is all there is to it.'

There were more theories and more revelations. For the first time, the newspapers mentioned a third member of Weston's unconventional household, an eight-year-old boy called Raymond Donaldson.

According to the New York Times, the couple had adopted the boy after his whole family died in the Spanish flu pandemic of 1918, but another newspaper referred to his family's deaths as 'mysterious'. Possibly this other family was not so much mysterious as mythical and in truth the child was Edward and Annie's own, born to Annie in her early forties. Weston's great-granddaughter recalls that family rumour suggested he had at least one love-child.

As time went on, a new theory developed about the incident. In July, a local newspaper claimed that there had been no attack at all, that the whole thing was a publicity stunt. A police sergeant who had investigated the case told the paper that there were discrepancies in Weston and Annie's stories and that a witness had seen a letter from Weston to his sister telling her not to worry, that nothing had happened.

By then Weston had recovered from his wounds but he and Annie and Raymond left the farm, and the area, for good. Weston told the *New York Times*, 'I will never sleep in this place again, but I won't sell it either. I am going to keep it for the boy.'

Whatever actually happened at the farm in Ulster County, Weston was never the same again. In April 1926 he was said to be living in Huntingdon, Pennsylvania, where he spent his time writing and replying to letters, 'queries he receives about hiking from all over the country', and he talked about another walk to the west coast. But just two months later a policeman found the 87-year-old wandering and incoherent in New York. He was identified by newspaper clippings he had in his pocket and was taken to the 'psychopathic' ward at Bellevue Hospital, where he was described as suffering from 'partial amnesia and senile psychosis'. After resting a while, Weston was lucid enough to tell doctors that he lived at 635 Indiana Avenue, Philadelphia. Police contacted Annie, who ran a small shop at the same address. She said that Weston had gone missing a few days ago and that she thought he might have walked all the way.

Another two months later, in August, Weston went missing again and Annie asked New York police to search for him. He was found four days later sitting on the steps of a house in Brooklyn, dressed in a blue suit, a shirt and tie and with two dollars in his pocket. He told Patrolman Brown: 'Why, if you had not found me when you did I might have walked to the coast without anybody knowing of it.' Weston was taken to the Gates Avenue Police Station and telegrams were sent to Annie and to his sister, who lived in Providence. Weston told police that a car had brought him to New York, but he could not remember anything else.

Annie told a reporter: 'He has been making his home with me and no doubt was aware that I have been doing my best to take care of both of us from my meagre earnings of the store. This fear of poverty drove him away. He has been proud and it worried him that he could no longer earn much money by walking.'

The next year, in February 1927, Edward, Annie and Raymond had moved to New York and Weston was reported to be looking for a job as a messenger to 'save himself and his adopted daughter from starvation'. A few weeks later, journalists discovered them living in a 'tiny, dingy flat' at 238 West 13th Street in New York's Lower East Side. Edward was said to be bed-bound following a stroke. The news brought a flood of donations of money and food and even an offer of a job. Annie said, however, that he could not take up the offer, that she 'was afraid

Mr Weston might not be able to remember directions and might get lost'. The New York Press Club stepped in to help the former reporter and appointed a committee to raise funds to help Weston.

On 13 March, two days before his 88th birthday, the *Times* revealed that Weston had 'received a birthday present that will enable him to live in comfort for the rest of his days'. Anne Nichols, a playwright and producer, had set aside a pension of $30,000 which would afford him $150 per week for the rest of his life. Anne Nichols' most famous play, Abie's Irish Rose, had been ridiculed by critics but spent five years on Broadway and made its writer wealthy. Weston celebrated his birthday and thanked Nichols for her generosity at a party at the Press Club on Spruce Street, with Annie and Raymond at his side.

Weston was greatly relieved to have security for himself and his family. A week after his birthday, on a rainy Sunday, Weston was walking to church with Raymond. When he was younger Weston had said that he was not religious, though he kept the sabbath for his mother's sake, but some time in his later years he converted to Catholicism, perhaps influenced by Annie. That morning he was on his way to give thanks for the change in his luck, and as he and Raymond walked, he chatted to the boy, reminiscing about his career. As they approached the corner of 11th Street and 7th Avenue, he was oblivious to the traffic. Someone shouted a warning but it was too late as Weston stepped off the pavement into the path of a cab. On the wet road the car could not stop quickly enough to avoid him and Weston was hurled back onto the pavement, where he lay crumpled.

The driver lifted the old man into his taxi and drove him to hospital, where he was x-rayed and treated for a head wound. The doctors were afraid that the injury he had suffered might prove fatal for a man of Weston's age and infirmity. He improved through the night, but remained in a confused state all the next day and 'babbled of the days of his hikes'. By evening, he was beginning to regain his senses. He was kept in his hospital bed for a few weeks, his mind frequently journeying away from the present and from his recent impoverished years to visit happier memories, especially his long walks in England and America.

In the middle of April, Weston was allowed to leave hospital and moved to a comfortable apartment, 250 Taaffe Place, Brooklyn, where Annie was to care for him. In June he withdrew a charge of assault against the driver, who agreed to settle the case out of court. By then, Weston's walking days were done; once he left hospital he was largely confined to a wheelchair. By the end of 1928 he had become bedridden, although on his 90th birthday, 15 March 1929, he was photographed with Annie, standing to cut his birthday cake. Weston stares into the camera. He has the austere expression of the properly confused; he looks like a man who has little idea where he is or why he is being required to cut this cake. Annie stands with him, smiling a little and keeping careful watch of the frail man beside her who once walked alone across deserts and through blizzards.

Edward Payson Weston died of old age on Sunday 12 May 1929, with Annie and Raymond at his bedside. After he died, the endowment created for him by Anne Nichols passed to a charity and, with the Great Depression on its way, Annie and the 13-year-old boy were left to manage alone. After his death, Annie explained to newspapers that Weston had not formally adopted her, and the papers referred to her now as his secretary.

Weston had once reckoned that he had walked more than 90,000 miles in his career, not including the distances he walked on his days off. He was, for a time, one of the most famous men in the western world and had shaken the hands of presidents, lords and legends. He worked so hard to be famous and to be respected for his achievements, but after his death his name faded quickly from the newspapers and from history. By the time he died the world had moved on, pedestrian competitions were part of a quaint old America like velocipedes and floor-length skirts; baseball and football had conquered all.

The name Edward Payson Weston had attracted doubt and controversy far more times than he would have liked, and before he disappeared into the past there was to be one more dispute. Weston was buried at St John Cemetery in Queens three days after his death. The *Brooklyn Eagle* made the shocking claim that Anne Nichols had saved Weston from a pauper's grave, that she had bought a plot for him at the cemetery and he would otherwise have been buried in a common plot in the Potter's Field on Hart Island in Long Island Sound. The paper also noted that 75 people were present for the funeral mass at St Patrick's Church, Brooklyn, including Annie and Raymond, Annie's sister Mary, Weston's daughter Maud and her two daughters, and a man called Leon Salmon, the oldest surviving member of the New York Press Club.

The pastor of St Patrick's, John F. Cherry, was furious. In a letter to the editor of the *Eagle*, he wrote that the reporter was sensation-seeking, no better than an ambulance chaser, and that the people of his parish had welcomed Weston to the church and would have 'saved the remains of this reputable old man from Potter's', even without Nichols' help, or else Weston's family would have done it, or the undertaker.

Cherry ended his letter on a sad note for Weston. The pastor emphasised that there were not 75 people at the mass, there were double that, but 'they were not there on account of Mr Weston. They did not know him ... The mourners were very few.'

In Weston's last years his mind retreated frequently to his triumphant walks in England and America — he could be there in the time it took to shut his eyes. But it was nearly 20 years since half a million people had filled Broadway to watch his final miles home from California, more than 50 since he had filled the Agricultural Hall in London with 20,000 people. He had outlived his friends and his rivals; the mourners were very few.

EPILOGUE

ED WESTON IS BURIED IN THE ST JOHN CEMETERY, Middle Village, New York, also the final resting place of congressmen, a mayor and a senator; of John J. Gotti of the Gambino crime family; of the artist Robert Mapplethorpe; and of a variety of other politicians, mobsters and creative types. In death as in life, he shares his world with a broad church of characters.

Just four miles east, and still in the borough of Queens, the world's longest certified foot race takes place each year. The 'Self-Transcendence 3,100 Mile Race' has no direct connection to Weston but it maintains a spirit that he embodied.

On 50 consecutive days each summer, runners in the ST3100 cover the equivalent of more than two marathons a day between 6 a.m. and midnight to reach their target in the allotted time. Other 'ultra-distance' competitors around the world typically take on challenges of between 100 and 1,000 miles.

Yiannis Kouros, born in Greece in 1956 and now based in Australia, has held every outdoor record between those distances at some point. Kouros represents a direct link back to the pedestrians of the Victorian heyday; in 1984, after 96 years, he broke the six-day record of 623 miles set in 1888 by Weston's contemporary and rival George Littlewood.

Other renowned modern-day ultra-distance athletes include Frenchman Serge Girard, who has walked without a day off across each of North America, South America, Australia, Africa and Europe; and Britain's William Sichel, whose day job of selling hand-dyed Angora thermal clothing subsidises a sporting life in which he has set more than 32 records in races up to 1,000 miles long.

Weston's more conventional sporting descendants can be found taking part in one of the 500-plus large-scale 26-mile marathons, staged in major cities from London to Paris to Berlin to Mumbai to New York and all points in between, involving tens of thousands of runners at a time.

Mass participation rather than mass spectatorship is now the order of the day. Quite why the great age of pedestrianism as a spectacle fizzled out so quickly is open to conjecture, but it burned most brightly for as short as a decade from the mid-1870s before fading.

Maybe there was an element of public distaste, in the end, to the suffering of some competitors and the whiff of corruption related to the inevitable gambling.

More likely, other organised sports established themselves and then held sway as organised leagues took root and half-day Saturdays for the working man became more common from the 1880s, freeing up part of the afternoons to watch sport.

Baseball took off as an organised sport in the US in that

decade, while the Football League in England held its inaugural season in 1888–89 and football never looked back.

We can only guess at what Ed Weston would make of our modern sporting world, with all its hype. Then again, he was a master of that, and was in other ways ahead of his time. He promoted healthy eating. He promoted temperance. He warned of the dangers of smoking and a sedentary lifestyle. He walked the walk, and then some.

BIBLIOGRAPHY

Books:

Peter Ackroyd, **Dickens** (1990)

Ray Allen Billington and Martin Ridge,
Westward Expansion: A History of the American Frontier
(University of New Mexico Press, 2001)

Hugh Brogan, **The Penguin History of the USA** (Penguin, 2001)

Edwin G. Burroughs and Mike Wallace, **Gotham: A History of
New York City to 1898** (Oxford University Press, 1999)

David Carlyon, **Dan Rice: The Most Famous Man
You've Never Heard of** (PublicAffairs, 2001)

Henry Steele Commager (ed.), **Documents of American History**
(Appleton-Century-Crofts, 1949)

Claude S. Fischer, **Made in America: A Social History of American
Culture and Character** (University of Chicago Press, 2010)

Michael Emery and Edwin Emery, **The Press and America**
(Simon and Schuster, 1992)

Joyce Litz, **The Montana Frontier**
(University of New Mexico Press, 2004)

PS Marshall, **King of the Peds** (Authorhouse 2008)

Edward Payson Weston, **The Pedestrian** (New York, 1862)

Maria Weston, **The Weeldon Family or Vicissitudes of Fortune**
(Boston, 1848)

Silas Weston, **Four Months in the Mines of California**
(Providence, 1854)

Jerry White, **London in the 19th Century** (Vintage Books, 2007)

Howard Zinn, **A People's History of the United States** (2005)

BIBLIOGRAPHY

Newspapers and magazines:

New York Times

Strength magazine

Turf, Field & Farm magazine

Chicago Tribune

New York Mail

Appleton Post Crescent

Providence Journal

Boston Journal

Rochester Democrat & Chronicle

Davenport Daily Gazette

Troy Times

British Medical Journal

Brooklyn Daily Eagle

National Police Gazette

The Penny Illustrated

Wellington Evening Post

New York World

Oakland Tribune

Poughkeepsie Eagle News

Auburn Citizen

New York Globe

Harper's Weekly

Sporting Life

Portsmouth Daily Herald

Dubuque Daily Herald

The Scotsman

New York Herald

Utica Daily Observer

Providence Evening Press

Titusville Morning Herald

Cleveland Herald

National Intelligencer

The Sportsman

Islington Gazette

Philadelphia Times

Forest and Stream

Bell's Life

Boston Globe

Syracuse Herald

Buffalo Express

Decatur Review

PHOTO CREDITS

Page 129:
A young Ed Weston, c.1867
Reproduced with the kind permission of John Weiss

Page 130:
top: A poster depicting Weston's 1,200-mile walk
from Portland to Chicago, 1867
Reproduced with the kind permission of John Weiss

bottom: The Daily Graphic, New York, 16 May, 1874
Authors' collection

Page 131:
top: A poster advertises a six-day walk
'Weston against the world', December 1876
Reproduced with the permission of Islington Local History Centre

bottom: The Illustrated Sporting & Dramatic News
Reproduced with the kind permission of John Weiss

Page 132:
Poster advertises Weston's first head-to-head with
the Irish-American maverick, Daniel O'Leary, London, 1877
Reproduced with the permission of Islington Local History Centre

Page 133:

top: The Graphic, 14 April 1877 dedicates its front page
to the Weston-O'Leary match
Authors' collection

bottom: The Daily Graphic, 21 June 1879
Authors' collection

Page 134:

top: A cartoon from the Daily Graphic, August 1879
Authors' collection

center: Weston at ease away from the track in 1879
Reproduced with the kind permission of the New York Public Library

bottom: Weston in England after completing a 5,000-mile temperance
walk in 1884, The Graphic, London, March 1884
Authors' collection

Page 135:

top: Weston on his trans-America walk from LA to New York, 1910
Reproduced with the kind permission of John Weiss

bottom: The Boston Daily Globe, May 1910 cartoon of the excitement
in New York when Weston finishes his coast to coast walk
Authors' collection

Page 136:

top: Weston with officials from the College of the City of New York,
2 June, 1913
Reproduced with the permission of the Library of Congress

bottom: Edward Payson Weston doffs his hat to his public
Reproduced with the permission of the Library of Congress

INDEX

Acknowledgement:

Sincere thanks to Joyce Litz, Ed Weston's great-granddaughter, for kind and enthusiastic support and for sharing family memories and documents. We hope we have done Ed justice.